THE PORTRAIT OF A LADY

Maiden, Woman, and Heroine

TWAYNE'S MASTERWORK STUDIES

Robert Lecker, General Editor

THE PORTRAIT OF A LADY

Maiden, Woman, and Heroine

Lyall H. Powers

Twayne Publishers • *Boston*
A Division of G. K. Hall & Co.

Twayne's Masterwork Studies No. 78

Copyright 1991 by G. K. Hall & Co.
All rights reserved.
Published by Twayne Publishers
A division of G. K. Hall & Co.
70 Lincoln Street
Boston, Massachusetts 02111

Copyediting supervised by Barbara Sutton.
Book production by Janet Reynolds.
Typeset by Compset, Inc., Beverly, Massachusetts.

10 9 8 7 6 5 4 3 2 1 (hc)
10 9 8 7 6 5 4 3 2 1 (pb)

The paper used in this publication meets the minimum requirements
of American National Standard for Information Sciences—Permanence
of Paper for Printed Library Materials, ANSI Z39.48-1984. ∞™

Printed and bound in the United States of America.

Library of Congress Cataloging-in-Publication Data

Powers, Lyall Harris, 1924–
    The portrait of a lady : maiden, woman, and heroine / Lyall H.
Powers.
        p.   cm.—(Twayne's masterwork studies ; no. 78)
    Includes bibliographical references and index.
    ISBN 0-8057-8066-1 (alk. paper).—ISBN 0-8057-8550-7 (pbk. :
alk. paper)
    1. James, Henry, 1843–1916. Portrait of a lady. I. Title.
II. Series.
PS2116.P63P62   1991
813'.4—dc20   91-11381

Contents

Note on the References
and Acknowledgments

Henry James's novel *The Portrait of a Lady* was first published as a serial; it ran in two different magazines, one English and one American, at the same time: from October 1880 to November 1881 in *Macmillan's* magazine and from November 1880 to December 1881 in the *Atlantic Monthly*. Then at the end of 1881 it was published in book form by Macmillan in London and by Houghton Mifflin in Boston. James made some minor revisions in the serial for book publication. With little further change, *The Portrait of a Lady* was published as the opening novel (the first three volumes) of the "Collective Edition" of James's works by Macmillan in 1883.

A quarter of a century after that first version of *The Portrait of a Lady* in 1881, James revised it thoroughly for the New York Edition of his novels and tales published by Charles Scribner's Sons between 1907 and 1909; it appeared in 1908 as volumes 3 and 4. James revised most of his early work for this edition—all that was to be included, that is—but none so extensively as *The Portrait of a Lady*. The revisions are in many instances so radical that some critics argue that there are really two James novels with the same title and that the heroine of each is, coincidentally, named Isabel Archer. The two versions are different, to be sure; but there are also important fundamental similarities. To a great extent, the purpose of the revisions was to clarify and give sharper emphasis to James's original intentions as he recognized them in the 1881 edition. It might be argued, then, that the 1908 revision is *The Portrait* that *The Portrait* was meant to be.

That revision was undertaken when Henry James was at the

Note on the References and Acknowledgments

height of his artistic powers, most critics agree. Critical discussion of the novel almost always focuses on the 1906 version. Consequently, the revised version is the one most often reprinted in paperback and other inexpensive editions for modern readers. In this study I have used the Norton Critical Edition of *The Portrait of a Lady*, edited by Robert D. Bamberg (New York: W. W. Norton, 1975). It is, of course, a reprint of the 1906 version, and includes the preface James wrote for volume 3 of the New York Edition; it also includes some excerpts from James's notebooks and from other relevant writings of his, some reviews of the initial publication of the novel in 1881, a selection of subsequent critical essays on the novel, and—particularly useful—an exhaustive list of textual variants, that is, the passages from the 1881 version that James altered or replaced in 1906. All quotations from *The Portrait* in this edition are referred to simply by page number(s) in parentheses; citations of other material included in this edition are referred to as NCE, followed by page number(s).

Also cited in the text is *Henry James Letters,* edited by Leon Edel, 4 vols. (Cambridge: Harvard University Press, 1974–84), by the abbreviation *Letters,* followed by volume and page numbers. *The Complete Notebooks of Henry James,* edited by Leon Edel and Lyall H. Powers (New York: Oxford University Press, 1987), is cited in the text as *Notebooks,* followed by page number(s).

I am grateful to Professor Leon Edel for permission to use two pictures of Henry James from his collection; to the Harvard University Library for permission to use a facsimile of a page from Henry James's notebooks; and to Geoffrey Spinks Bagley, Esq., Honorary Curator of the Rye Museum, Rye, East Sussex, England, to use a picture of Henry James's Garden Room, Lamb House, Rye.

Portrait of Henry James, 1900, by his cousin Ellen "Bay" Emmet Rand. (Private collection of Leon Edel)

Chronology:
Henry James's Life and Works

1843	Henry James born 15 April at 2 Washington Place, New York City, a second son to the religious philosopher Henry James and Mary Robertson (née Walsh) and brother to William, born 11 January 1842.
1843–1844	At age six months, Henry is taken to Europe with the family. He always maintained that his earliest memory was of being driven in a carriage across the Place Vendôme in Paris. That experience is perhaps the foundation of the international theme in his fiction.
1845–1846	Two more brothers born: Garth Wilkinson James on 21 July 1845, and Robertson James on 29 August 1846. Family moves to Albany, N.Y.
1847–1848	Family moves to a large house, 58 West 14th Street, New York City. A sister, Alice James, born 7 August 1848.
1848–1855	Henry receives an irregular education at various day schools in New York City; he becomes an "inveterate" theatergoer and a "devourer of libraries." He begins writing.
1855–1858	James family returns to Europe because Henry James, Sr., wants his children "to absorb French and German and get a better sensuous education than they are likely to get here [in the United States]." Henry is educated at schools in Geneva, London, Paris, and Boulogne-sur-Mer and by private tutors.
1858	Family returns for a brief sojourn in Newport, R.I.—always a favorite location for Henry as an ideal compromise between America and Europe.
1859	Back in Europe with his family, Henry attends school in Geneva and learns German in Bonn.
1860–1861	Family returns to Newport. Henry studies painting (as does William) with William Morris Hunt. While serving as a vol-

unteer fireman, Henry seriously strains his lower back—an "obscure hurt," he calls it. (Hemingway later starts the rumor that the "hurt" was emasculation, caused by Henry's bicycle or horseback riding!) Two younger brothers serve with the Union Army in the Civil War.

1862–1863   Henry spends one term at Harvard Law School; he attends lectures but devotes his attention to James Russell Lowell's lectures on English literature and Old French, to reading Sainte-Beuve, and to his own writing.

1864   Achieves his majority. Family moves to Boston, then to Cambridge. Henry publishes his first short story ("A Tragedy of Error") and first critical essay (on Sir Walter Scott).

1865–1869   Establishes himself as a reviewer in the *North American Review, Atlantic Monthly,* the *Nation,* and *Galaxy*—with 56 reviews, most of them unsigned; also as short story writer—11 during the period, six in 1868 and three in 1869.

1869–1870   Takes first trip alone to Europe, having planned to meet in Italy in the spring with his beloved cousin Mary ("Minny") Temple. Minny dies early in 1870, but remains a kind of muse figure for Henry, and her spirit "haunts" him for the rest of his life.

1870–1871   Back in Cambridge, Henry begins friendship with William Dean Howells. His first novel, *Watch and Ward,* is serialized in the *Atlantic Monthly.*

1872–1874   Henry accompanies his sister Alice and Aunt Kate to Europe for the summer of 1872; he remains there, visiting Paris and Rome before returning to New York.

1875   Publishes his first collection of tales, *A Passionate Pilgrim,* first collection of travel pieces, *Transatlantic Sketches,* and first novel in book form, *Roderick Hudson,* and makes first attempt at expatriation by moving to Paris. There he meets the group of French writers he calls "the grandsons of Balzac"— Flaubert, Zola, Daudet, Maupassant, and others—as well as the Russian expatriate Ivan Turgenev.

1875–1876   Moves to London's Piccadilly—3 Bolton Street; visits France and Italy; continues to write fiction and criticism.

1877–1879   Publishes his first collection of critical writings, *French Poets and Novelists,* and his first best-seller, the novella *Daisy Miller*; also the novels *The American* and *Watch and Ward* and the novella *The Europeans*; and his first literary biography, *Hawthorne.* With election to the Reform Club and the Athenaeum, his social life expands notably.

Chronology: Henry James's Life and Works

1880–1881   Publishes the novel *Washington Square*; his *The Portrait of a Lady* begins to run serially in an English and an American magazine almost simultaneously and continues through 1881.

1881–1883   Comes back to the United States in October to visit in Washington, D.C. His mother dies in February 1882; in May, James returns to London and crosses to France. News of his father's illness brings him home again—just too late, as his father dies during the week before Christmas. Henry James—no longer "Jr."—serves as executor. In August 1883 he returns to England to begin his definite expatriation. Collective Edition of his fiction is published in 14 volumes.

1884–1886   Renews friendship with "the grandsons of Balzac" and begins his experiment with realism and naturalism by publishing his important essay "The Art of Fiction." Brother Garth Wilkinson dies in Milwaukee; sister Alice joins Henry in England. James moves from Piccadilly to 34 De Vere Gardens, Kensington, near Robert Browning. Bourget dedicates his novel *Cruelle Enigme* (1885) to Henry. James publishes *The Bostonians* and *The Princess Casamassima* in 1886.

1887–1890   Has long sojourn in Italy; friendship with the Daniel Curtises begins; friendship with Constance Fenimore Woolson blossoms. He meets Kipling. *The Tragic Muse* (1890), intended to be his "last long novel," ends the decade of experiment in realism-naturalism; he turns *The American* into a play.

1891–1895   The theatrical experiment with *The American* enjoys a modest success; of James's next four plays only *Guy Domville* is produced (1895), its author being booed the first night. He returns to his "own old pen" of fiction. Alice dies in 1892. Fenimore Woolson dies in 1894, perhaps a suicide; Henry feels responsible.

1896–1898   Publishes *The Spoils of Poynton* and then *What Maisie Knew*, which begins a series of stories of threatened children—*The Turn of the Screw* follows in 1898. Writer's cramp obliges him to begin dictating to a typist. He moves into Lamb House, Rye, Sussex.

1899–1901   Enjoys friendship with the sculptor Hendrik Andersen. Publishes *The Awkward Age* and *The Sacred Fount*. Meets writers Joseph Conrad, Ford Madox Ford (then Hueffer), Stephen Crane, and H. G. Wells—for whom he becomes "The Master."

1902–1904   In successive years publishes *The Wings of the Dove*, *The Ambassadors*, and *The Golden Bowl*. Begins long friendship with Edith Wharton; meets Jocelyn Persse.

1904–1905   Revisits the United States for a long lecture tour, which revives memories of Newport and Minny Temple. Arranges with Scribner for a collective edition of his novels and tales, the New York Edition.

1907–1909   Publishes *The American Scene* and the New York Edition. Suffers from nervous depression.

1910   Brother William and wife visit Rye; both brothers are ill. Henry returns to the United States with William, who dies in August; youngest brother, Robertson, dies. Henry's last tale ("A Round of Visits") and last collection of tales (*The Finer Grain*) are published.

1911–1912   Receives honorary doctorate from Harvard. Returns to Lamb House. Publishes his last novel (*The Outcry*), begins his autobiography, and receives an honorary doctorate from Oxford.

1913   Moves into Chelsea flat, 21 Carlyle Mansions. His seventieth birthday is commemorated by the gift of a golden bowl from English friends, a portrait by Sargent, a bust by Derwent Wood, and an invitation (15 April) to the Prime Minister's at 10 Downing Street. Publishes *A Small Boy and Others* (autobiography I).

1914   Publishes *Notes of a Son and Brother* (autobiography II) and his last collection of criticism (*Notes on Novelists*). Vigorously involved in war work, he lends his Watchbell Street studio for the use of Belgian refugees, visits the wounded at St. Bartholomew's Hospital, and serves as chairman of the American Volunteer Motor Ambulance Corps.

1915   Helps Edith Wharton with *The Book of the Homeless* for war fund. Disappointed by continuing U.S. neutrality, James becomes a British subject, 26 July. On 4 December he suffers the first two of a final series of strokes; has steadily fewer lucid intervals.

1916   On 1 January is awarded the Order of Merit, the highest civilian decoration. Dies, 28 February. His funeral is held in Chelsea Old Church, his ashes buried in the family plot in Cambridge, Mass. His last publication, the preface for Rupert Brooke's *Letters from America*, appears. At death, James left incomplete two novels, *The Ivory Tower* and *The Sense of the Past*, the third autobiographical volume, *The Middle Years*, and a book on the great city, "London Town" (as he called it in his notebooks).

1976   Commemorative tablet honoring James unveiled in Poets' Corner of Westminster Abbey, 17 June.

LITERARY AND
HISTORICAL CONTEXT

1

The Place of *The Portrait of a Lady*

The world into which Henry James was born was in the grip of the industrial revolution. Science had rediscovered and embraced the experimental method—a system of seeing for oneself instead of following obediently the established beliefs of one's predecessors. Experiment made possible the technological developments that changed the world from being mainly agricultural to predominantly industrial, from relying on manpower to relying on the horsepower of machines. The new science led men like Charles Darwin to those discoveries he published in *On the Origin of Species* (1859). Such works called seriously into question the reliability of the biblical account of creation and therefore shook the very foundations of religious faith. With that, the whole question of the importance of "authority" cried out for reexamination and redefinition.

The James household and its immediate milieu reflected these revolutionary tendencies. Henry James, Sr., was a friend of Ralph Waldo Emerson, the urgent advocate of self-reliance and independent-mindedness who found even Unitarianism too authoritative a religious system for his taste. To a considerable extent Henry James, Sr., shared the ideas of Emerson. Both men were attracted to the religious philosophy of the Swedish mystic Emmanuel Swedenborg (1688–1772), and not least because of his warning against following established religious ritual, heeding the dictates of religious authority. The senior James was also interested in the poet William Blake (himself influenced by Swedenborg), who was sharply critical of the "mind-forg'd manacles" of religious and political institutions alike. That strongly Protestant attitude characterizes the tradition of the poet John Milton as well as Blake, certainly, and appears in American literature in the fiction of Nathaniel Hawthorne, who was a very important influence on the younger Henry James.

The Emersonian idea of self-reliance figures prominently in the educational system—or lack of it—from which Henry James, Jr., drew benefit. Regular schooling in his native America was minimal; he attended a variety of schools in Europe, was put into the hands of tutors, and left to pursue his own interests in libraries—which, his father reported, he "devoured." Father James wrote to Emerson when his sons William and Henry were aged seven and six respectively to say that he was taking the boys to Europe, where they could get a "better sensuous education than they are likely to get here." That attitude was responsible for the protracted trans-Atlantic shuttle that took the young Henry so frequently to Europe; by the time he reached the age of seventeen he had spent about a third of his life abroad and had fully absorbed what he called the "European virus." In this feature of his early experiences lies the basis of a pervasive theme in James's fiction, doubtless the most typical and important, and certainly a dominant characteristic of *The Portrait of a Lady*—the international theme.

The American in Europe was a phenomenon readily encountered during the latter half of the nineteenth century, and James commented on it to his family frequently and fully during his first solo journey abroad. None of those comments is more telling than that in a letter of 13 October 1869 from Florence to his mother; he begins by comparing Americans and the English but soon turns to a general observation on his countrymen. "A set of people less framed to preserve self-complacency . . . it would be hard to imagine," he announces: they are vulgar, ignorant, and stingy-minded. "On the other hand, we seem a people of *character*, we seem to have energy, capacity and intellectual

4

The Place of The Portrait of a Lady

Photograph of Henry James, 1880s. (Private collection of Leon Edel)

stuff in ample measure. What I have pointed at as our vices are the elements of the modern man with *culture* quite left out. It's the absolute and incredible lack of *culture* that strikes you in common travelling Americans." "The pleasantness of the English," he concludes as he returns to his original comparison, is due to the fact that "They have manners and a language. We lack both" (*Letters,* 1:152). The American, in a word, is incomplete, and that incompleteness not only proclaims itself in the European setting but seems liable to be corrected—in the alertly receptive—by the qualities of that environment.

Another similar comment based on his experiences during that first trip—this one to his brother William—amplifies the passages just quoted and clarifies the whole matter of James's attitude, especially as it relates to *The Portrait of a Lady.* "Now that I am in England," he says, he has a further word of praise for the qualities of the American character: "As for the [English] women . . . I revolt from their dreary

5

deathly want of—what shall I call it? Clover Hooper has it—intellectual grace—Minny Temple has it—moral spontaneity. They [the English] live wholly in the realm of the cut and dried" (*Letters*, 1:208).

James's terms of evaluation—and particularly "moral spontaneity" as opposed to "the cut and dried"—sound rather Emersonian. The young woman to whom that term is applied, a cousin to Henry James, needs a special word. Minny Temple was something very like the love of his life (although he specifically denies this in a letter to his brother William; the denial itself is quite instructive, like protesting too much), and her memory "haunted" him to his old age. He and Minny had planned to join each other in Italy in the spring of 1870 and together complete his first solo journey in Europe. She died of tuberculosis, however, at about the moment of James's writing to William in praise of her "moral spontaneity." She was just twenty-five. Her influence on James's fiction was significant—most obviously in *The Wings of the Dove* and certainly in *The Portrait of a Lady*. Friends wrote to him to claim that they recognized Minny in Isabel Archer, heroine of *The Portrait*. His response was an ambivalent yes and no.

News of Minny's death prompted revealing responses from James in his letters home. Two themes persist: (1) he felt Minny did not really belong to this earthly realm, and (2) she was for him an inspiration and a guide—and something more. Though he refused to mourn her death, he explains to William,

> there is nothing sadder than this view of the gradual change and reversal of our relations: I slowly crawling from weakness and inaction and suffering into strength and health and hope: she sinking out of brightness and youth into decline and death. It's almost as if she had passed away—as far as I am concerned—from having served her purpose, that of standing well within the world, inviting and inviting me onward by all the bright intensity of her example. (*Letters*, 1:224)

He has very nearly claimed that Minny's death was sacrificial.

The memory of her "moral spontaneity" guided James in the creation of the heroes and heroines of his "international fiction": "She was," he insists to William, "a breathing protest against European grossness, English compromises and conventions—a plant of pure American growth" (*Letters*, 1:228). There is a further qualification, however, as James associates Minny specifically with Newport, Rhode Island—his beloved cousin with his favorite geographic location. To his mother: "I think of Newport as with its air vocal with her accents, alive with her movements" (*Letters*, 1:222); and to William: "The whole past—all times and places—seem full of her. Newport especially—to my mind—she seems the very genius of the place" (*Letters*, 1:226). Newport is America, all right, but America with a difference, perhaps more rounded, finished, and complete. This association of Minny and Newport has particular significance for an understanding of James's international fiction, and especially of *The Portrait of a Lady*.

James's delight in Newport is everywhere apparent in his writing, early and late, for it represented to his mind quite simply the acceptable compromise between America and Europe, a successful union of those qualities he found to admire in the English and their way of life (or in the Europeans generally) with those he cherished in his compatriots. And Minny Temple was the *genius loci* of Newport, "the very genius of the place." James's development of the international theme in his fiction seems to be a constant quest for that very compromise, union, fusion between the European and the American. That international confrontation was his constant metaphor, the *means* of expression he used again and again in his literary career. It is significant to note that he published a second essay on Newport ("The Sense of Newport," *Harper's Magazine*) in 1906, the very year in which he was busy revising *The Portrait of a Lady*.

There were of course other female figures than Minny Temple in his mind, literary heroines with whom he had been familiar for a long time: Jane Austen's Emma Woodhouse (*Emma*, 1816), Charlotte Bronte's Jane Eyre (1847), Gustave Flaubert's Emma (*Madame Bovary*, 1857), and George Eliot's Gwendolyn Harleth (*Daniel Deronda*, 1874) and Dorothea Brooke (*Middlemarch*, 1871), as well as Hawthorne's Hester (*The Scarlet Letter*, 1850) and Miriam (*The Marble*

Faun, 1860). These literary heroines are strong-willed young women, admirably or regrettably confronting the challenges typically presented by social custom to members of the "weaker sex" who legitimately aspire to a broader range of options than the roles of mother and housewife or brittle spinster. As such, they anticipated the contemporary concern with the "new woman," who was beginning to assert herself as a personage to be reckoned with during the last quarter of the nineteenth century, and the women's movement for reform.

James's career spanned the literary development of a century even though his publishing life extended only from 1864 to 1916. It began under the influence of romanticism, pursued the experiments of realism and naturalism, and finally helped prepare the way for the psychological fiction of such modern masters as Marcel Proust (who died in 1922), James Joyce (d. 1941), and William Faulkner (d. 1962). James's first essay in literary criticism was focused on the fiction of Sir Walter Scott, the prolific Scottish romantic; James's earliest American master was Nathaniel Hawthorne, who also belongs in the tradition of romance. Interestingly enough, however, James chose for special praise Scott's talent at realistic depiction, his ability to show us "men and women . . . in their habits as they lived." And in spite of his obvious indebtedness to his American master, James complained (in his literary biography *Hawthorne*, 1879) that the author of *The Scarlet Letter* was not enough of a realist. James claimed as his own "greatest master" the French realist Honoré de Balzac, creator of a multitude of actors in the human comedy. To the end of his career James was constantly concerned with the most effective means of depicting reality; his attempts are a kind of history of the novel.

By the time James published his literary biography of Hawthorne he had already published three substantial novels, romantic rather than otherwise, and two of them—*Roderick Hudson* (1875) and *The American* (1876)—along with his best-selling novella *Daisy Miller* were his first major ventures developing the international theme. He had also published nearly three dozen tales, two other novels, a volume of criticism, and scores of literary reviews. He had met a number of important writers such as George Eliot, the English realist, and Flaubert, Zola, Daudet, Maupassant, and Turgenev—the "grandsons of Balzac," as he called them. In those first fifteen years of his career he had begun to master his craft. The artisan starts out as an apprentice—to use the old terminology of the craft unions—on the long road to learning his craft; when he has become sufficiently adept at the practice he focuses all his talent and learning on the creation of a piece that will admit him to the rank of master. That creation was called the "master-piece." In that strict sense of the term, *The Portrait of a Lady* was James's master-piece. He knew it would be from the outset.

The publication of the novel during the year 1880–81 helped mark a crucial moment in James's life. In the short space of three years he lost both his parents and his younger brother Wilkie as well as the old family friend Ralph Waldo Emerson. Admired fellow-artists in fiction Gustave Flaubert and George Eliot died in 1880, and Ivan Turgenev in 1883, the year in which James turned forty. On the death of his father he began to sign his work "Henry James"—not "Junior," as he had previously signed it: he was now the senior Henry.

He returned, a definite expatriate, to England in August of 1883. The following year he published his most important single essay, "The Art of Fiction." He devoted himself to a series of three novels, experiments in the realist-naturalist mode of Zola and Daudet (and even of George Eliot), and then gave five years to the experiment of writing for the theater—unsuccessfully, indeed traumatically. He found compensation for that trauma, however, in what the experience of writing for the stage did for him as an artist: "the precious lesson, taught me in that roundabout and devious, that cruelly expensive way, *of the singular value for a narrative plan too* of the . . . divine principle of the Scenario . . . a key that, working in the same *general* way fits the complicated chambers of *both* the dramatic and the narrative lock . . ." (*Notebooks*, 115). He would henceforth make his fiction dramatic, that is, *immediate* in its presentation to the reader—like that of a play on the stage to its audience—without the interference of the mediating explanatory and omniscient author. And what he would chiefly dramatize in his fiction would be the *psychological* adventures of his heroes and heroines.

The twentieth century began with publication of James's triple triumph, *The Wings of the Dove* (1902), *The Ambassadors* (1903), and *The Golden Bowl* (1904)—a stunning achievement, enough for an average writer's lifetime. He returned for a year to America, for a lecture tour, and while there arranged with Charles Scribner's Sons for publication of the New York Edition of his novels and tales—including *The Portrait of a Lady*, to which he gave extensive revision between 1906 and 1908.

When the First World War broke out and England entered in August 1914, James threw himself into support of the Allied cause with all the energy and dedication he could muster. There was some sense of compensation there for his having failed to participate actively in the United States Civil War fifty years earlier. Bitter disappointment over the failure of his native land to come at once to the aid of Britain, France, and Belgium prompted James to renounce his American citizenship and to become a British subject in the summer of 1915. Thus ended the lifelong love-hate affair with America. A sweet irony perhaps lies in the fact that James's achievement in fiction stands as a glowing tribute—in spite of all—to Columbia, gem of the ocean.

2

The Importance of
The Portrait of a Lady

The attraction of *The Portrait of a Lady* for all kinds of readers—and therein lies its signal importance—is surely due to the heroine James has created. There are two points to be noticed in this claim: (1) the heroine, Isabel Archer, what she is and does and what she finally becomes; (2) James's creation of her, his exposition, expression, and presentation of Isabel. Of course. Behind this simple account, however, lies all the complex quality of that interesting young woman, her believable humanity, the familiarity of her situation, and the relevance of her problems; and the extraordinary talent that has gone into the depiction of Isabel and her career to enable us readers to experience all those qualities—as though she were an actual person. The evident and necessary combination of these two elements—content and form, if you like—accounts for James's successful achievement and our continuing interest.

Isabel's mixture of brashness and timidity, of a strong desire— almost a compulsion—to see life for herself and yet a reluctance to risk fully responsible commitment, of precocious wisdom and immature folly, all that enables us to recognize in her something of ourselves. She earns our sympathy first by her openhanded frankness and personal honesty, and at least our pity when she finds herself bound in a life-threatening situation that seems to offer no easy escape. In many ways she is more foolish than those around her; yet she is liable to strike readers as being a better person (whatever that means—but I suppose most of us would agree!) than all those others. Certainly Ralph Touchett thinks so; in fact most of the characters in the novel seem to think so, even though they do not all respect her for her "goodness."

What is apt to strike the average reader of *The Portrait* is that *nothing happens:* in the tradition of adventure stories, Isabel Archer has no adventures—nor have any of the other characters. But James asks us, tacitly and implicitly, to reconsider our notion of "adventure." What happens in the mind and what happens *to* it, he implies, is what most matters in life. Isabel and the others in the novel have their share of psychological adventures. One of the features of the 1908 revised version of *The Portrait* is the increased amount of attention given to Isabel's psychology, to her consciousness of what is happening in her life. What Isabel *is* acquires more importance than what she *does.* That should not really be so surprising: we all tend to be interested in the private life of a celebrity, we say we want to know what he does when he is not on the field, what she does when she is not on stage; but what we mean is that we want to know what the celebrity is really like when out of the limelight and not on public show. James's fiction speaks directly to that curiosity.

Between the 1881 version and the 1908 revision of *The Portrait of a Lady* James's experience as a writer led him to experiment with the means of making his expression of his characters' psychological processes more effective. He was much influenced by Flaubert's insistence that a story be as lifelike as possible, that the storyteller be kept as much out of sight as possible, that the story seem to come to the reader as directly and immediately as the action of a play on the stage—or of life itself. Don't let the story seem "made up" and the storyteller a manipulator. James's experience of writing for the theater, from 1890 to 1895, encouraged him to see the virtue of this approach to writing fiction. Actually the principle behind that adjuration is one

Photograph of the interior of the Garden Room of Lamb House, Rye, where Henry James revised *The Portrait of a Lady* in 1906–7; it was destroyed by German bombs in 1940. (Rye Museum Association Photographic Collection; Geoffrey Spinks Bagley, honorary curator)

that American humorist Mark Twain had discovered and employed successfully as a public speaker—one that anyone who likes to tell jokes knows very well: don't give it away, don't "explain" it, be subtle and leave something for your audience to do, present your joke in such a way as to let them "get" it.

Successful joke-telling and effective storytelling, then, need careful preparation and arrangement of the material involved: the good joke and the good story must in a way tell themselves. Nobody *tells* a play (except in such rare cases as, say, Thornton Wilder's *Our Town*); the stage play tells itself. With this idea, then, we come to the whole matter of "narrative technique," of how to create a story that will be *self*-expressive. This includes everything from the overall shape of the story, the arrangement of its constituent parts and the establishing of relations among them, down to the very small matter of choosing exactly the right word in any given instance. It involves the use of items of expression that mean more than themselves, that are rich in connotative value—symbols, figures of speech (especially synecdoche), double entendre, and so on—and the meaningful grouping and juxtaposition of characters and events. The 1908 revision of *The Portrait of a Lady* paid careful attention to the sharpening of such means.

James was so successful, even in the 1881 version, at not explaining away his story, at being subtle, at leaving plenty for his readers to do, that many of them complained he had left the novel unfinished. What is the point of the end of the novel? What really will Isabel do? What has happened? That was the kind of question they asked. The significance of the ending and what it does to the meaning of the whole novel has fascinated generations of readers: what exactly is this lady once her portrait is finished and what does it tell us about her psychological makeup and development? The arguments continue.

Whatever it means, Isabel's portrait is indeed a portrait—even though a literary portrait. That means we watch, over time (as we read), the creation of that portrait. Fiction is a plastic art, a temporal concern, whereas portraits are usually static and their structure a spatial affair. James does recognize that the creation of this portrait is certainly developmental, time-consuming, yet he clearly wants his readers to consider this portrait as somewhat spatial, as existing outside—or in spite of—chronological flux. The greatest artists have always strained against the limits of their artistic medium; painters try to get a sense of temporality into their work (the cubist Picasso is a good example) or writers try to get a sense of spatial development into their work (Joyce and Proust are good examples). How to express contemporaneity, simultaneity?—that is their common problem. James's technique for the depiction of Isabel in *The Portrait of a Lady* is to emphasize what she finally *is*, what she *has become*. It is as though James had taken a length of movie film, a strip of frames usually seen in sequence, and arranged it so that we finally see all the squares simultaneously, one upon the other. T. S. Eliot later did the same thing in his portrait of J. Alfred Prufrock: as we follow the opening invitation—"Let us go then, you and I / . . . Let us go and make our visit"—we come to realize that we are viewing and participating in *all* the visits that Prufrock has ever made to the room where the women come and go and talk of Michelangelo, simultaneously. James too focuses our attention less on the sequence of events than on the cumulative psychological effect they exercise upon Isabel Archer.

Finally, what James has to say about humanity, the human condition, the morality of human relationships—with oneself as well as with others—counts for a great deal in the appeal of *The Portrait of a Lady*. In spite of disagreement about what exactly Isabel has become and what the ending of the novel means, readers recognize in it an accurate depiction of human good and evil. It is not a question of "moral message" in any narrow or oversimplified sense, not a matter of moralism but rather a matter of profoundly serious morality: James is concerned with what truly enhances human existence (that is, with "good") and with what diminishes it (that is, with "evil"). He phrases the questions "What is good?" and "What is evil?" in ways that accommodate the complexity of such questions and that do not dishonor the reader's serious pondering of them.

Pondering such questions amounts to confronting the problem of how to live. For Isabel Archer (as for all James's heroes and heroines, really) that problem phrases itself in terms of freedom and necessity— or rather the conflict between them: one cannot hope to enjoy absolute freedom. One cannot do or be (in spite of earnest claims to the contrary) all that one might want, and not only because of one's physical and mental limitations. The society one lives in, for instance, imposes limits on one's behavior: how one may dress, what actions are acceptable in public and what must be kept private, how one expresses oneself both verbally and with gestures, even the ways one thinks about things. Yet we are free to question those traditions and conventions of society; in fact we *ought* to do so. If we understand and accept certain traditions, conventions, laws—if we can see why they are "good" for us (and not the reverse of that) individually and collectively—then we have made them ours. We thus enjoy a participatory freedom. St. Paul had something like that in mind when he claimed that the true Christian is above the law; so, evidently, had Virgil's

Aeneas when he announced "I am glad to follow the will of the gods." This is different from "doing your duty" as a soldier must. James was in fact quite opposed to that concept of duty; he favored the concept of doing one's duty to oneself, in as fully enlightened a way as one can manage. His fiction argues, implicitly, that true maturity consists in examining life and oneself honestly, in accepting the necessary limitations and exercising one's consequent freedom fully. James has depicted the human condition honestly, has taken into account the complexity of human beings and made his fictional characters faithfully complex, and he has consistently refused to simplify the problems that a complex civilization presents or to offer simplistic solutions to them. He has successfully sustained the illusion that he is presenting the whole human scene, in a given story, quite impartially. That accomplishment continues to intrigue and engage and satisfy the great variety of readers who come to *The Portrait of a Lady* looking for a broad and deep view of life—looking for serious entertainment.

All these features of Isabel Archer's story combine to account for the importance of *The Portrait* and for its enduring interest to readers. These features were already present in large part in the 1881 version; they are enriched and matured and their expression is sharpened and weighted in the revision of the novel published in 1908.

3

Intention, Realization, Reception

Henry James seems to have been blessed with clairvoyant prevision about *The Portrait of a Lady* from almost the earliest moment of its conception: he foresaw its importance and he foresaw what would be taken for its weaknesses. He initially conceived of it as a feminine version of his novel of 1877, *The American*. He referred to his projected heroine as "an *Americana* . . . a female [Christopher] Newman" (*Letters*, 2:72); he knew it would be not only a "big" novel but a "great" novel and would demand of him plenty of time to be handled properly. He was confident that it would differ from his earlier work not just in degree but in kind.

In *The Portrait of a Lady* James resumes the evident opposition established in *Roderick Hudson* and *Daisy Miller*, not the American versus the European but the American versus the *Europeanized* American. The difference is of considerable importance for at least two related reasons: first, it helps make clear that James's novel is not merely a fictionalized sociological study of two conflicting cultures, the American and the European; and, second, that the whole arrangement of introducing an American into the European milieu is fundamentally a literary metaphor for expressing his ideas about how one reaches civilized human maturity.

James anticipated readers' objections to *The Portrait:* too much psychology, too little action, and a cropped ending. On this last, his defense was ready:

> The obvious criticism of course will be that it is not finished—that I have not seen the heroine to the end of her situation—that I have left her *en l'air* [up in the air, suspended].—That is both true and false. The *whole* of anything is never told; you can only take what groups together. What I have done has that unity—it groups together. It is complete in itself—and the rest may be taken up or not, later. (*Notebooks,* 15)

The remarks of contemporary reviewers of the new novel by Henry James show that his prevision was accurate, although understandably not quite so extensive as it might have been. *The Portrait of a Lady* was not uniformly well received in England, even though a number of reviewers who had some objections to the novel recognized it as a serious achievement. But in the United States it enjoyed a generally good reception. W. C. Brownell reviewed it for the *Nation* in February 1882 (he was soon thereafter made literary consultant for Scribner's) and called it a masterpiece. John Hay's review for the *New York Tribune* (25 December 1881) praised the novel: "Of the importance of this volume there can be no question. It will certainly remain one of the notable books of the time. It is properly to be compared, not with the light and ephemeral literature of amusement, but with the gravest and most serious works of imagination which have been devoted to the study of the social conditions of the age and the moral aspects of our civilization." And it is worth mention that in the first six weeks after its publication American sales totaled 2,937 copies.

British reviewers were more severe in their criticism of the novel's ending than James had anticipated, but he did not foresee the stunningly odd turn of that criticism: they found the ending immoral. Henrietta Stackpole's concluding remark in the novel, "'Look here, Mr. Goodwood,' she said; 'just you wait!'" was taken as a promise that Isabel was ready to accept an illicit liaison with Caspar. The reviews of Margaret Oliphant and R. H. Hutton (both reprinted in the Norton

Critical Edition) illustrate this response. James's notes indicate that his intention was quite what the finished novel realized: "he beseeches her to return with him to America. She is greatly moved . . . but she refuses. She starts again for Italy" (*Notebooks,* 15).

The expected objection to overpsychologizing was voiced by critics on both sides of the Atlantic. Ironically, some critics accurately noted James's intention without realizing what they had in hand. Mrs. Oliphant complained of the depiction of Isabel, "we have to receive both herself and her immediate surroundings, not so much as they actually are, but as they are seen through her eyes" (NCE, 657). The more perceptive and generous Horace Scudder gets even closer to seeing what is going on:

> The characters, the situations, the incidents are all true to the law of their own being; but that law runs parallel with the law which governs life, instead of being identical with it. . . . Only when one is within the charmed circle of the story is he under its spell, . . . the introversion which now and then takes place deepens the sense of personality. In that masterly passage [Chapter XLII] . . . the reader seems to be going down as in a diving-bell into the very secrets of her nature. (NCE, 653)

Critics were responding, willy-nilly, to James's achievement in psychological realism.

Perhaps most exciting of all critical responses to the 1881 *Portrait* is the anonymous review in *Harper's* (February 1882). It anticipates, in the comparison of painter and novelist, an important feature of James's essay of 1884, "The Art of Fiction": "*The Portrait of a Lady,* by Henry James, Jun., fulfills all the technical conditions that are essential for the production of a perfect portrait in oil, save those that are mechanical or manual, and manifests clearly enough how successfully the pen may compete with the pencil in the sphere of pictorial art" (NCE, 654).

Henry James must have had in mind, at some level of consciousness, the variety of critical response that these representative quotations illustrate when he undertook the revision of *The Portrait of a*

Facsimile of a page from Henry James's notebooks anticipating "the obvious criticism" of *The Portrait of a Lady*. (Harvard University Library)

Lady in 1906. It seems perfectly evident that his aim in working to improve the novel involved the clarification of his original intentions. In the intervening quarter of a century since the original version was published James had devoted his efforts to the development of both the theory and the practice of the art of fiction. Two examples of his revision might be mentioned at once to indicate how they are calculated to address again what he had originally anticipated as likely objections to *The Portrait*. He attempted to refine and strengthen his depiction of Isabel Archer's psychological makeup and to extend and sharpen his use of her point of view (literally speaking)—the presentation of "both herself and her immediate surroundings . . . as they are seen through her eyes," as reviewer Oliphant expressed her amazed perception of Isabel's situation. On many occasions James took the opportunity to change terms like "sense," "notion," and "idea" to "consciousness," and verb phrases like "it seemed" and "it appeared" to "she thought" or "she was conscious of" and so on. The second feature of the revision addresses especially the mysteries of the conclusion of the novel, and it does so in two ways: James has augmented the imagistic expression of his narrative by making concrete and palpable what had been comparatively abstract and vague; with that he has altered images to create related networks, changed some figures of speech to create extended metaphors, and replaced symbols to make them conform with each other and create a unified symbology out of merely random symbolism. The point of this aspect of the revision is that those less obvious features of the novel, which tend to influence the reader quietly, subtly, unobtrusively, almost without one's noticing them, are very important means for the author to express his ideas and realize his intentions—without being preachy, pointed, obvious.

Changes in the passages describing Lord Warburton's proposal of marriage to Isabel in chapter 12 illustrate the replacement of an abstract and vague account with concrete and specific imagery.

> 1881: These words were uttered with a tender eagerness which went to Isabel's heart, and she would have given her little finger . . . But though she could conceive the impulse, she could not let it operate; her imagination was charmed, but it was not led captive. What she finally. . . .
>
> 1908: The words were uttered with a breadth of candour that was like the embrace of strong arms—that was like the fragrance straight in her face, and by his clean, breathing lips, of she knew not what strange gardens, what charged airs. She

21

would have given her little finger . . . But though she was lost in admiration of her opportunity she managed to move back into the deepest shade of it, even as some wild, caught creature in a vast cage. The "splendid" security so offered her was *not* the greatest she could conceive. What she finally. . . . (99–100)

Another set of revisions calculated to create a linked network of imagery adds emphasis to Isabel's consciousness of the masculinity, the phallic quality of the rejected suitors Lord Warburton and Caspar Goodwood. In its focus on Warburton's riding crop, this scene is matched by the revised depiction of Goodwood. For example, chapter 33 of the 1881 version describes him as "Straight, strong and fresh," whereas the 1908 version alters this to "Straight, strong and hard" (276).

This increased emphasis and sharpened focus lend particular force to a slight revision in chapter 42 as Isabel recalls her earliest times as Mrs. Osmond and the dire change that ensued. In 1881, James wrote: "It had come gradually—it was not till the first year of her marriage had closed that she took the alarm." And 1908: "It had come gradually—it was not till the first year of their life together, *so admirably intimate at first,* had closed that she had taken the alarm" (356). The added phrase, which I have italicized, gains emphasis from the preceding revision of "her marriage" to "their life together," and this alteration in turn gains in significance from the new phrase. The cumulative effect of this network of revisions exerts considerable influence on our reading of the closing scene of the novel and Caspar's augmented kissing of Isabel: there James adds (among much more), "she felt each thing in his hard manhood that had least pleased her" (489).

There are two available sources of information about what guided James in his revision of *The Portrait of a Lady*—in addition, of course, to the testimony of the revisions themselves: (1) specific references in letters and in the preface to the novel, written for the New York Edition of it (1908), and (2) critical statements about fiction generally, made both prior to and contemporaneously with revision of the novel. First, from a letter to the Scribner publishers (12 June 1906) about the extensive revision of the earliest volumes of the New York Edition—*Roderick Hudson, The American,* and *The Portrait:* "what I have just been doing for the 'Portrait' must give it a new lease of such life as it may still generally aspire to" (*Letters* 4:408–409).

His most important single statement of his artistic theory is the long essay "The Art of Fiction." Because he was at the moment of publishing this essay about to embark on an extended experiment with writing realistic fiction, seeking to do something in the style of Zola and the other "grandsons of Balzac," and (with luck) to gain his kind of popularity and income, it is hardly surprising that the essay has the appearance of a Realist Manifesto. He compares the creator of fiction to the painter and demands of the writer an accurate rendering of life; he insists on "the importance of exactness—of truth of detail"; he confesses that "the air of reality (solidity of specification) seems to me to be the supreme virtue of a novel"; and he explains that "It is here in very truth that he [the writer of fiction] competes with life, it is here that he competes with his brother the painter in *his* attempt to render the look of things. . . ." Clear enough, so far—and sufficient to make Horace Scudder say (one would imagine) "That's my point exactly!" But as we follow on to the completion of James's sentence we encounter a qualifier that profoundly alters the significance of the explanation—and would reconfound poor Scudder: "to render the look of things, *the look that conveys their meaning*" (my italics).[1] And with that, all is said.

James's point is that it is futile to pile detail upon detail with the aim of showing how things really look without managing to make these details *expressive* and *representative*—without, that is, selecting and arranging them to answer the question "What does all this *mean?*" The key to James's intention lies in his choice of terms: "The only reason for the existence of a novel is that it does attempt to represent life" (*Criticism,* 1:46). Not "reproduce" but "represent": the distinction here is the same as that between the typical photograph that tries to catch the object *as it really looks* and the artistic one that tries to capture the significance, the meaning, the essence of the object.

In spite of some critics' objections to the 1881 version, and even in spite of his own observation that the novel "is too exclusively psychological . . . depends too little on incident," James in fact strengthened the emphasis on his heroine's consciousness in the revised version. He did little to increase "incident" or action or "adventure," at least as those terms were traditionally understood (and often still are). The idea for *The Portrait of a Lady* began, he recalls, with his conception of his heroine, Isabel Archer, as "a certain young woman affronting her destiny . . . an intelligent but presumptuous girl" (NCE, 8). The next question was what to do with her, how to make her "a Subject": " 'Place the centre of the subject in the young woman's own consciousness,' I said to myself, 'and you get as interesting and as beautiful a difficulty as you could wish. Stick to *that* for the centre . . . her relation to herself' " (NCE, 10–11). He still had, however, to confront the question "What will she 'do'?" (NCE, 14). The answer he provided is of signal importance, for it marks the crucial step from traditional realism to psychological realism; and that is not simply the transition from depicting "the look of things" to selecting "the look that conveys their meaning," but onward to portraying the whole affair of *apprehending that meaning*. Such apprehending, James claims, is "adventure."

To illustrate this claim, James selects the scene in chapter 42— "the young woman's extraordinary meditative vigil"—and comments, "it throws the action further forward than twenty 'incidents' might have done. It was designed to have all the vivacity of incident and all the economy of picture . . . a representation of her motionlessly *seeing*" (NCE, 15). (James had prepared this answer twenty years earlier, in "The Art of Fiction," when he raised the question "And what *is* adventure . . . ?" His answer was simply, "A psychological reason is, to my imagination, an object adorably pictorial; . . . There are few things more exciting to me, in short, than a psychological reason" (*Criticism*, 1:61).

•   •   •

Intention, Realization, Reception

The pendulum swings of critical and scholarly attention to James since his death have been instructive; that attention burgeoned after the Second World War and has blossomed profusely in the last twenty years. It was a commonplace of early criticism to couple him with writers like William Dean Howells and to view his fiction as typical "comedy of manners" literature. Howells had himself coined the phrase "the international theme" to account for James's novels like *The Portrait of a Lady* by indicating that their main concern was sociocultural, a comparison of American and European society—their conventions, manners, and traditions, or lack of them. Thus it was deemed important for serious readers to be made aware of the historical, philosophical, and social context that gave rise to James's fictions; the stories themselves were often regarded as a kind of special historical artifact. A salutary adjustment was provided by the rise and extension of the New Criticism (between the two world wars), which demanded close attention to the literary work itself as an artistic construction and thus having its own rules of organization and arrangement—as one might deem a portrait by Sargent worthy of attention *not* because of its subject but rather because of its artistic ordering and expression, the *rendering* of its subject.

The New Critics (the first generation of whom, at least, were also real scholars) followed what they saw as James's critical precepts and examples; James's fiction attracted them because it was evidently fashioned according to those principles. In 1943, the New Critical journal the *Kenyon Review* devoted a whole issue to James. The general result of New Critical attention was that the international theme, the placing of an American character like Isabel Archer in a European setting to see what she would "do," was regarded as an elaborate metaphor—something like what T. S. Eliot called an "objective correlative"—however thick, rich, and complex that surface story appeared to be.

In the past quarter of a century the pendulum has swung back, attention has been returned to the surface of the story and to the historical, philosophical, and sociocultural context it reflected. Initial impetus to that swing was undoubtedly given by Leon Edel's exemplary biography of James (1953–72) and his complementary edition of James's letters (1974–84)—the impetus of a thorough and far-ranging scholarship and of the pioneering use of psychoanalytic advances in both biography and literary explication (further augmented by his *Stuff of Sleep and Dreams*, 1982). Related biographical studies followed and further developed Edel's pioneering in psychobiography: Jean Strouse's life of sister Alice James (1980), Howard M. Feinstein's life of brother William (1984), Jean Maher's of the two younger James brothers (1986), and Alfred Habegger's several studies of Henry James, Sr. (in the *Henry James Review* during the 1980s). There has also been a proliferation of studies that might be called neohistorical in that they direct attention to the actual setting out of which the story of Isabel was drawn and against which it must be seen to be fully appreciated. A clear sense of this approach is given by a sentence in Alfred Habegger's preface to his *Gender, Fantasy, and Realism in American Fiction* (1982):

> The critic has to find out certain things about the world that received the text—has to discover the books that were in the air at the time, the sort of people who read and liked these books, the social divisions within the reading public and the configuration of genres that appealed to these groups, the stereotypes of men and women that happened to be getting a lot of attention, and most important of all, the exact state of the ongoing concern about the nature of womanhood.[2]

Examination of "the books that were in the the air" when James first published *The Portrait* argues persuasively that James was well aware of what was popular among the mainly female audience, tried to some extent to emulate the best-sellers while "correcting" the facile and romantic wish-fulfilling representation of life that led to happy endings. Such examination has been made by William Veeder, Anne T. Margolis, and Joseph Allen Boone (see Bibliography), as well as by Habegger. James's alertness to the economics of his profession and his attempt to compete (especially in his *Portrait*) with the best-sellers is documented in Marcia Jacobson's *Henry James and the Mass Market*

Intention, Realization, Reception

(1983) and Michael Anesko's *"Friction with the Market": Henry James and the Profession of Authorship* (1986).

James's awareness both of the predominance of women in his reading public and of the rising movement in support of the emancipation of women and the emergence of the emancipated "new woman" has been thoroughly noted, beginning with the essays by Annette Niemtzow and Nina Baym and the books by Judith Fryer (1976), Virginia C. Fowler (1984), and Elizabeth Jean Sabiston (1987) listed in the Bibliography. And a good example of the importance of understanding *The Portrait* in terms of its contemporary political background is Cheryl B. Torsney's 1986 essay "The Political Context of *The Portrait of a Lady*" (see Bibliography).

This kind of attention helps us to understand the context in which the novel was conceived and developed and gives us a good grasp of what materials were available to James in his creation of the story; this approach tends to favor the 1881 version of *The Portrait* largely because it seems more "realistic" (see especially Baym and Habegger) and to reflect more immediately the context out of which the novel arose. It is somewhat less helpful in explaining what the novel means, what James's use of the available materials manages to express. A refreshing and maybe surprising alternative is offered by the Marxist critic Annette T. Rubinstein, that "James was *not*, essentially, the sort of traditional realistic novelist he wished and thought himself to be." She argues that James's best works "involve, in varying degrees, a kind of symbolism, running all the way from morality play to myth, which makes the individuals involved stand for some group or force quite beyond their personal selves, and thus allows James to break out of the claustrophobic circle of a consumers' value system into which at worst he often falls."[3] And the problem of the ending of the novel, of Isabel's decision to return to Rome, remains unenlightened for the most part by the neohistorical approach. Anne Margolis's informative chapter on *The Portrait*, for example, clearly explains how the ending successfully avoids the conventional conclusions of popular fiction: "Isabel Osmond's . . . return to Rome . . . can be attributed to James's determination to escape the twin literary tyrannies of contemporaneous English and French fiction, the happy and the 'indecent' ending."[4] Such a reading, however, tells us little of what Isabel's career—her experiences and her development—has to say to the reader.

Textual criticism of the past twenty-odd years has increasingly benefited from such related disciplines as psychology (psychoanalytic theory), anthropology, linguistics, and philosophy.[5] The best of it is devoted to explanation of what the novel means, what it is all about, what it expresses through the thick and rich surface *story*. And the most satisfactory addresses the subject James foresaw would most engage critical readers, the ending: the objection "that I have not seen the heroine to the end of her situation—that I have left her *en l'air*." Current criticism does not always object to the ending but ponders, rather, what it does to the meaning of the whole story. Some critics think Isabel is just returning to "the safety of her celibate marriage with Osmond," others think she has gone back to "face the music" or "pay the piper," others that she wants to be faithful to her moral obligations—her marriage vows or her promise to Pansy; still others gather up all the possible explanations (and more) as though to suggest that there is merit in each; for example, "One does not really know where that straight path leads Isabel—to Italy to escape the passion which still seems the greatest threat to her freedom, to keep her promise to Pansy, to buy her freedom from Osmond, or to make the best of her self-made prison."[6] Such readings, however, seem to disregard the text of the novel itself, to overlook the very terms James employs to characterize Isabel's career and convey his fundamental concerns—even though he labored manfully and artistically to make those concerns clearly manifest in his revision of *The Portrait*.

Most useful, I think, are those studies of the novel that attempt to find an appropriate set of terms *equivalent* to James's in order to "translate" the novel into another—and more available because (it is hoped) more familiar—idiom. Tony Tanner appeals to the distinction made by Kant between "value" and "worth," that is, between what one can put a price tag on and what cannot be measured in dollars, pounds, or francs. Annette Larson Benert offers an illumination of *The Portrait* in terms of the psychology of Carl Jung, especially his theories of nature and the psychic. More recently, Paul B. Armstrong has given an extended phenomenological reading with the help of the ideas of Heidegger and others in *The Phenomenology of Henry James* (1983), and Virginia C. Fowler adapts the psychology of Jacques Lacan in her *Henry James's American Girl* (1984). Finally, a small group of critics, noting James's place in the tradition of Protestant Christianity, that of Milton, Blake, and Hawthorne, for example, has tried to use those terms to "translate" the novel into an equivalent idiom. This last group includes the early and little-noticed essay "*The Portrait of a Lady:* 'The Eternal Mystery of Things'" (1959).

It might be productive to see what these "equivalent idiom" approaches have in common and how a consideration of their mutual relevance serves to illuminate the ending of *The Portrait* and the dominant themes developed throughout the novel that lead to that ending—virtually inevitably—and so clarify what the novel is all about, what it "means." I will undertake that exercise in the ensuing chapters.

A READING

4

Miss Archer and Mrs. Osmond

A critical reading of *The Portrait of a Lady* might begin with the lead provided by James's preface. He says there that "the germ of my idea" consisted "not at all in any conceit of a 'plot,' nefarious name," but "altogether in the sense of a single character, the character and aspect of a particular engaging young woman, to which all the usual elements of a 'subject,' certainly a setting, were to need to be super-added" (4). The emphasis is on the importance of character, of the engaging young Isabel Archer, but we note the distinction made between character and plot—that is, between picture and action or *stasis* and movement—although James recognizes the need for both.

The novel opens with careful preparation for the effective dramatic entrance of the main character: the scene is an almost ideal setting for the ceremony of afternoon tea, and all the gentlemen present are anticipating the arrival of the interesting girl from America. They know she is "quite independent," but aren't sure what *that* means. She makes her dramatic entrance, framed for a moment in the doorway leading to the garden, all eyes focused upon her; she remains the focus of the story. The dramatic—or theatrical—mode continues as James allows Isabel to characterize herself by her words and actions; he himself gives very little interpretive comment.

The three gentlemen are immediately taken by her, and even the dogs are at once captivated, as though they sympathize with her natural goodness. She quickly proves herself to be innocent and naive and charming as well as independent-minded. Her romantic outlook is revealed when cousin Ralph introduces her to Lord Warburton and she responds, "Oh, I hoped there would be a lord; it's just like a novel!" (27). The note of independence is soon sounded as the question of the length of her visit is raised. She first replies, appropriately, "My aunt must settle that"; then—

> "I'll settle it with her—at a quarter to seven." And Ralph looked at his watch again.
> "I'm glad to be here at all," said the girl.
> "I don't believe you allow things to be settled for you."
> "Oh yes; if they're settled as I like them." (29)

And as Ralph suggests that Mrs. Touchett has adopted her, Isabel remarks that she is "not a candidate for adoption": "I'm very fond of my liberty" (30).

In the next three chapters of flashback the character of Isabel is given historical substantiation; we are introduced briefly to the young man in Isabel's life, Caspar Goodwood, in terms that we will recall frequently in the course of the novel: "he was a straight young man from Boston . . . tall, strong and somewhat stiff" (42). There is also a sketch of Ralph, an American who was educated in England as well, thus "English enough," but "His outward conformity to the manners that surrounded him was none the less the mask of a mind that greatly enjoyed its independence, on which nothing long imposed itself" (43–44). Independent-minded Ralph is an apt cousin and friend for Isabel—and the novel will test that appropriate relationship. Ralph early confesses to his mother that Isabel "strikes me as very natural" (48); yet he soon has further evidence of her "natural" romanticism, with which he must contend as he shows her about the house. She asks, "isn't there a ghost?" He assures her that it is "not a romantic old house," but Isabel insists on the ghost. And we attend to that because there may be more than romance involved here. Says Ralph: "I might show it to you, but you'd never see it. The privilege isn't given to every one; it's not enviable. It has never been seen by a young, happy, innocent person like you. You must have suffered first, have suffered greatly, have gained some miserable knowledge. In that way your eyes are opened to it. I saw it long ago" (52).

It is tempting to call Isabel a typical American—James might seem to be doing so—and to categorize her as "Emersonian."[7] She is fond of her freedom and of making her own choices, apparently self-reliant. Yet there is another side to Isabel, inescapably: with all her independent-mindedness there is a certain reluctance to confront life. We remember her thanking Mrs. Touchett for telling her she should not sit alone with gentlemen in the evening and other things one shouldn't do. "So as to do them?" asks her aunt. "So as to choose," is Isabel's cool reply (67). Yet we know that from her earliest years the reluctance to face experience, a kind of cherishing of her ignorance, has marked Isabel. She liked the office beyond the library, in her family home in Albany; but there was a bolted door there that gave onto the street: "But she had no wish to look out, for this would have interfered with her theory that there was a strange, unseen place on the other side—a place which became to the child's imagination, according to its different moods, a region of delight or of terror" (33). Although she claims to Ralph that she is fond of knowledge, he is correct in his response: "Yes, of happy knowledge—of pleasant knowledge. But you haven't suffered, and you're not meant to suffer. I hope you'll never see the ghost!" (52).

Isabel very soon finds herself the recipient of two proposals of marriage that present themselves to her (and even more so to us readers) as fundamentally similar. Caspar Goodwood and Lord Warburton are quite different individuals, obviously, but the salient and important features of their proposals are almost identical. There are three such features, and we have glanced at a couple of them already. Isabel sees marriage as a threat of diminished freedom: Warburton's proposal makes her feel like "some wild, caught creature in a vast cage" (100); and to Goodwood's proposal she responds with, "I like my liberty too much. If there's a thing in the world I'm fond of, . . . it's my personal independence" (142). There is more in that threat, however, than Isabel may be consciously aware of, although James makes it apparent to the reader; we have seen (in chapter 3) how the revisions are evidently calculated to emphasize the phallic quality of the two suitors—Warburton's agitated hunting crop, his "implement of the chase" (gaining in significance from the literary echo of *Madame Bovary*) and Goodwood's very person, "Straight, strong and hard" and the "disagreeably strong push, a kind of hardness of pressure, in his way of rising before her" (both revised to sustain this particular emphasis). The third common feature in the two proposals is the pleasant ambient atmosphere attendant upon each—the sense of "strange gardens . . . charged airs" and of "the bright air of the garden" (with revision bringing the two into line, as was noted in chapter 3). Surely that touch is an expression of the aroma of prelapsarian innocence, a whiff of the flowers of the original Garden of Eden before the satanic serpent lurking there got to the dwellers and made them aware of their (sinful) nakedness.

One difference between the two suitors for Isabel's hand is worth notice; that is the " 'splendid' security" offered by Warburton. He can offer her a choice of homes to live in; the one he takes her to visit enjoys the security of a protective moat but carries the ominous-sounding name of "Lockleigh," suggesting the ironic and oxymoronic modern term "maximum security." Another touch is added by Warburton's scarcely visible sisters, the Misses Molyneux, who are sweet and shy (73); the one Isabel likes best "had a smooth nun-like forehead and wore a large silver cross" (115). James makes sure that we don't miss the detail, as he continues the focus: "Isabel was sure moreover that her mild forehead and silver cross referred to some weird Anglican mystery—some delightful reinstitution perhaps of the quaint office of the canoness." The "religious imagery" of this passage forms part of a persistent theme in the novel, as we shall note.

An additional feature of Isabel's response to Warburton's proposal has to be recalled, for it too participates in a network of expression in the novel. As Warburton makes his case he ends with the plaintive "I don't see what more you can ask!" Her reply points up her evident wish—or at least her claimed desire—to escape dependence, to be allowed an equal share in the ventures that concern her: "It's not what I ask; it's what I can give" (99). And the question of charity, of her ability to give, rises again and again.

One of James's comparatively few explanatory comments on Isabel occurs in the opening paragraph of chapter 17: "That love of liberty of which she had given Caspar Goodwood so bold a sketch was as yet almost exclusively theoretic; she had not been able to indulge it on a large scale" (145). Ralph Touchett seems bent on correcting that unfortunate condition; and he is obviously delighted at her explanation of her rejection of Warburton's offer of marriage. (And at this point we see an important piece of the opaque surface of the novel—James's concern with the plight of women faced with a severely restricted range of opportunities.) "I don't see what harm there is in my wishing not to tie myself. I don't want to begin life by marrying. There are other things a woman can do" (133), Isabel claims. Ralph responds eagerly:

> "You want to see life—you'll be hanged if you don't, as the young men say."
> "I don't think I want to see it as the young men want to see it. But I do want to look about me."
> "You want to drain the cup of experience."
> "No, I don't wish to touch the cup of experience. It's a poisoned drink! I only want to see for myself."
> "You want to see but not to feel," Ralph remarked. (133–34)

Isabel remains ambivalent (at best) in her attitude to independence, self-reliance, and freedom. It is almost as though her fundamental desire is to hold herself suspended, uncommitted, unobligated by choice—and thus ignorant of the fact that the refusal to choose is itself a choice. In spite of all, however, Ralph will do everything he can to assure that Isabel gains the freedom he wants her to have—a freedom he tries to convince himself that she wants—by persuading his father to divert a large share of his own inheritance to Isabel, a fortune that will free her of material dependence. Before we leave this scene of their discussion of "seeing life," we must pause over Ralph's mild complaint to her, "You've a great many friends that I don't know. You've a whole past from which I was perversely excluded." Isabel's simple reply proves, in retrospect, to be heavy with significance: "You were reserved for my future" (130).

At the death of old Mr. Touchett Isabel inherits the substantial sum of £70,000. Should we expect Isabel to be delighted, for what does the money mean but the freedom Ralph intended it to be? In chapter 21 she almost challenges Ralph with responsibility for the inheritance (she is of course unaware of his persuasive role in it) and accuses him of frivolity: "Is that why your father did it—for your amusement?" (One still runs into misguided readers who think Isabel has got it just right!) Ralph turns serious and gives her a piece of advice, and in terms that are repeated often later: "Take things more easily. Don't ask yourself so much whether this or that is good for you. Don't question your conscience so much. . . . Live as you like best, and your character will take care of itself. . . . Spread your wings, rise above the ground. It's never wrong to do that" (192). His word of caution about questioning her conscience ought to remind us of the crucial scene in Twain's great novel in which Huckleberry Finn decides to do as his *conscience* bids him and write to Miss Watson that he has her runaway slave, Jim, with him; but Huck's "moral spontaneity" prevents him from sending the letter; he rips it up and declares (with Twain's sharp irony flashing) "All right, I'll go to hell." The innermost core of his being has asserted itself. Ralph is inviting Isabel to pay similar heed, to obey her moral spontaneity. Her response is sobering and terribly significant: "I'm afraid; I can't tell you. A large fortune means freedom, and I'm afraid of that" (193). But the gift has been bestowed; the freedom is now hers. The next step is to show what she does in consequence.

That next step has in fact already begun with her meeting Serena Merle. The first time we and Isabel see Madame Merle it is with her back turned to us as she plays the piano. An impressive scene, if we really look at it. She proves to be good with her hands—a good manipulator, as she will later acknowledge to Gilbert Osmond: "I don't pretend to know what people are meant for, . . . I only know what I can do with them" (207). She and Isabel have become friends, close enough for her to admire Isabel and to point out wherein she is deficient. Madame Merle explains, "You're an exquisite creature. . . . But speaking strictly, you know, you're not what is technically called a *parti* . . . you're not embarrassed with an income. I wish you had a little money" (176). What is behind this appraisal we discover when Madame Merle learns of Isabel's grand inheritance. That scene must be visualized if we are to appreciate its full effect (the hands; watch the hands):

> "A fortune!" Madame Merle softly repeated.
> "Isabel steps into something like seventy thousand pounds."
> Madame Merle's hands were clasped in her lap; at this she raised them still clasped, and held them a moment against her bosom while her eyes, a little dilated, fixed themselves on those of her friend. "Ah," she cried, "the clever creature!" (181)

The attitude of prayerful adoration before the specified sum (worth several times more then than now—say $1,500,000) is revealing, as is her comment on Isabel's "clever" achievement. Mrs. Touchett's sharp retort, "What do you mean by that?" brings an unaccustomed blush to Serena's cheek, and she extricates herself by modifying the comment to "clever to achieve such results—without an effort!" Now, however, Madame Merle can introduce the heiress to Gilbert Osmond and see them married.

The characterization of Serena not only portrays her as sophisticated, worldly, and conventional but so emphasizes these qualities as to make them appear decidedly unfavorable, threatening, perhaps evil. Furthermore, that emphasis illuminates her similarity to Gilbert Osmond. Chapter 19 shows the growing relationship between Serena and Isabel and augments the characterization of that sophisticated lady. Isabel admires her social ease: "It was as if somehow she had all society under contribution, and all the arts and graces it practised"

(166). Isabel is grateful for the friendship, but there remains a qualification: "She was in short the most comfortable, profitable, amenable
person to live with. If for Isabel she had a fault it was that she was
not natural; . . . that her nature had been too much overlaid by custom
and her angles too much rubbed away. She had become too flexible,
too useful, was too ripe and too final . . . too perfectly the social ani-
mal" (167). Ralph confirms Isabel's impression with extra emphasis
and with the same flourish of rhetoric, saying of Serena that "she
pushes the search for perfection too far": "She's too good, too kind,
too clever, too learned, too accomplished, too everything. She's too
complete, in a word" (216). (It is hard not to be reminded here of a
moral neatly pointed at the conclusion of Hawthorne's *The Scarlet
Letter*: "Be true! Be true! Be true! Show freely to the world, if not your
worst, yet some trait whereby the worst may be inferred!") We might
expect Isabel to ask her cousin if he means Serena is too good to be
true. Instead of that she says,

> "I suppose you mean by that that she's worldly?"
> "Worldly? No," said Ralph, "she's the great round world itself."
> (216)

The very phraseology of that summary we will recognize when it is
repeated with reference to Gilbert Osmond.

The contrast with Isabel is clear, for Isabel is certainly "natural,"
unworldly, and incomplete. It is important to add that she is also un-
conventional—or at least *not* conventional. Early in the novel Isabel
has told her uncle that "I'm sure the English are very conventional"
(59); he agrees that they are. Isabel adds: "I'm not in the least stupidly
conventional. I'm just the contrary" (60). When she rejects Goodwood's proposal of marriage, he says he will allow her a couple of
years for travel, and concludes, "I don't want you to be conventional"
(143). Her behavior, furthermore, illustrates that she is not that.

What Isabel finds in Gilbert Osmond is a gentleman of taste, of
unaggressive good manners: he is sophisticated, worldly, and conventional. His influence on Isabel is similar in kind to Madame Merle's

but rather different in degree. James characterizes him as he has Serena, but in a somewhat more elaborate way. His places of residence are appropriate, they suit him and, indeed, "express" him. (Those residences are not simply opaque features of the surface of the narrative.) Here is the look of Osmond's villa in Florence, the look that conveys its meaning: "The house had a front upon a little grassy, empty, rural piazza . . . this antique, solid, weather-worn, yet imposing front had a somewhat incommunicative character. It was the mask, not the face of the house. It had heavy lids but no eyes; the house in reality looked another way" (195). But it is not the suggestion of deceptiveness that strikes Isabel; her impression, on her first visit to the villa, is that "There was something grave and strong in the place; it looked somehow as if, once you were in, you would need an act of energy to get out" (217).

Once inside the place, Isabel responds to the influence of villa and master: so impressed is she that her famous naturalness and moral spontaneity threaten to forsake her; the effort to behave as she thinks she ought (for the first time!) tires her. "A part of Isabel's fatigue came from the effort to appear as intelligent as she believed Madame Merle had described her, and from the fear (very unusual with her) of exposing—not her ignorance; for that she cared comparatively little—but her possible grossness of perception. . . . She was very careful therefore as to what she said, as to what she noticed or failed to notice; more careful than she had ever been before" (226).

Perhaps the carefulness is a step in the right direction, toward the sophistication, worldliness, and conventionality she lacks. Her relationship with Osmond begins well, and he confesses to her frankly, "I was poor, and I was not a man of genius"—"I was simply the most fastidious young gentleman living. There were two or three people in the world I envied—the Emperor of Russia, for instance, and the Sultan of Turkey! There were even moments when I envied the Pope of Rome" (227). The confessed envy of the Pope is reiterated (252, 256), but not the reason he gives here for that envy: "I envied the Pope of Rome—for the consideration he enjoys." It is not surprising, then, that he sends his daughter, Pansy, to a convent to be educated, nor, indeed, that his most urgent expression of his attraction to Isabel occurs in the largest and most splendid of all the churches in Rome—in fact, in all the world—St. Peter's Cathedral. James adjusts the significant emphasis of that encounter most adroitly: "Isabel . . . found herself confronted with Gilbert Osmond, who appeared to have been standing at a short distance behind her. He now approached *with all the forms— he appeared to have multiplied them on this occasion to suit the place*" (252, my italics; original version: "approached with a formal salutation").

On her first visit to Osmond's villa, the "careful" Isabel not only notices that Osmond is a man of taste but also compares him to Ralph Touchett in this respect. The distinction she thus makes between the two men is a telling one—at least for us, at that moment: "He had consulted his taste in everything. . . . Ralph had something of that same quality, this appearance of thinking that life was a matter of connoisseurship; but in Ralph it was an anomaly, a kind of humorous excrescence, whereas in Mr. Osmond it was the key note, and everything was in harmony with it" (224–25). Isabel makes no evident appraisal here, but the distinction she details is sharpened later, in Rome, after Osmond's urgent appeal in St. Peter's and his subsequent confession of love for her. Isabel's plan is to leave Rome immediately with Mrs. Touchett; Osmond's gambit is to express agreement with the plan, and in so doing he sounds like Ralph Touchett: "Go everywhere, . . . do everything; get everything out of life," and finally, do "what you like" (262). Then comes his declaration, "I find I'm in love with you" (263).

Two observations are needed. First, Isabel reaffirms her own hesitancy when confronted by the need to commit herself to a choice; her response is regret and retreat, much "as she had retreated in the other cases before a like encounter," and once again she expresses "the dread of having in this case too, to choose and decide" (263). Second, the similarity between Osmond and Ralph is overwhelmed by their difference as the comparison serves to set up a distinct contrast—as had the earlier question of their being men of taste. Osmond continues his apparent agreement with Isabel's plan to leave: "Do everything that's proper. I go in for that. . . . you'll discover what a worship I have for propriety." But he has changed the tune a little, and Isabel is alerted:

> "You're not conventional?" Isabel gravely asked.
> "I like the way you utter that word! No, I'm not conventional: I'm convention itself." (265)

The phraseology distinctly echoes Ralph's comments to Isabel about Madame Merle: "Worldly? No, . . . she's the great round world itself." Denial of the qualifying adjective to assert the noun is reminiscent of the distinction made by Emerson in "The American Scholar" between the true man and the one who has sunk into, been overcome by, his particular function—"Man farming" as against the mere "Farmer." Emerson's point is that humanity loses its humanness when it commits itself wholly to a particular quality or function. So James would seem to be implying that in going beyond the worldly and the conventional, Serena and Osmond have been diminished as human beings. After her marriage, Mrs. Osmond will confront that possibility directly.

Serena is kept in our mind as we read of Osmond, as though James wanted to sustain the close association as a matter for close attention. Isabel's reluctance to face the choice presented by Osmond's proposal recalls an earlier discussion between her and Serena. Serena has reminded Isabel that it is all right for a girl to refuse "a few good offers" so long as they are not the best she is liable to get. Madame Merle adopts "the worldly view" (originally "that view") as she cautions Isabel, "don't keep on refusing for the sake of refusing. It's a pleasant exercise of power; but accepting's after all an exercise of power too" (176). Although the context quite clearly focuses on the danger of a girl's being left with no further marriage proposals (and what else can a girl hope for?!), the broader philosophical implications are there as well: not to choose is itself a choice, and choosing not to engage with life is a failure to live. Serena's observation is sound and useful advice. James is honestly faithful to the complexity of her personality; it has two sides, the sound and the unsound or dehumanized, and she is a comparatively sympathetic character, at least up to this point.

Similarly, her discussion with Isabel of convention contains its share of good points; the apportioned emphasis illuminates both women. The discussion has been anticipated by Isabel's summing up her impressions of Serena with the comment that she is "not natural" (167): "Madame Merle was not superficial—not she. She was deep, and her nature spoke none the less in her behavior because it spoke a conventional tongue. 'What's language at all but a convention?' said Isabel." That concluding question is to ponder. Madame Merle launches the subsequent discussion by observing that everyone has an expressive "shell," a "cluster of appurtenances" that represent him or her: "What shall we call our 'self'? . . . I know that a large part of myself is in the clothes I choose to wear. . . . One's self—for other people—is one's expression of one's self; and one's house, one's furniture, one's garments, the books one reads, the company one keeps—these are all expressive." Isabel denies the claim: "Nothing that belongs to me is any measure of me; everything's on the contrary a limit, a barrier, and a perfectly arbitrary one." She continues:

> "Certainly the clothes which, as you say, I choose to wear, don't express me; and heaven forbid they should!"
> "You dress very well," Madame Merle lightly interposed.
> "Possibly; but I don't care to be judged by that. My clothes may express the dressmaker, but they don't express me. To begin with it's not by my own choice that I wear them; they're imposed upon me by society."
> "Should you prefer to go without them?" Madame Merle enquired in a tone which virtually terminated the discussion. (175)

Before we join Huckleberry Finn in a rousing cheer for Isabel, we ought to pause long enough to see that the logic of her argument would lead her to answer "Yes!" to Serena's evidently rhetorical question. For it is the logic of innocence, the innocence that the biblical story of Adam and Eve presents in that naked pair before the serpent wriggles into the Garden. Yet there is something arresting and appealing in Isabel's taking into account the arbitrary effect of *things* (to mention only them) upon our independence and freedom. Here, however, is a problem indeed for her to confront: how to reconcile the wish for freedom with the recognized demands of *necessity?* For convention is merely one of the facets of necessity that combine to limit our liberty.

Isabel Archer marries Gilbert Osmond, "convention itself," against the wishes and advice of almost everybody (except Serena Merle). She has a baby but it dies in infancy. (Should one take this as a sign that nothing vital can be produced by the union of Isabel with Gilbert?) When Ralph pays his first visit to Mrs. Osmond he is impressed and depressed by the striking change that has occurred in his cousin; and what further impresses us readers is the choice of terms in which Ralph conveys that change—terms that recall Isabel's discussion with Serena about what expresses oneself. Ralph has seen nothing of Isabel during the two years since her marriage and fears that "As Osmond's wife she could never again be his friend" (327), that, in fact, "for him she would always wear a mask" (330). When Isabel receives him, she is prodigally overdressed and majestically ornamented:

> if she wore a mask it completely covered her face . . . it was a representation, it was even an advertisement. . . . She appeared to be leading the life of the world. . . . The free, keen girl had become quite another person; what he saw was the fine lady who was supposed to represent something. . . . she represented Gilbert Osmond. "Good heavens, what a function," he then woefully exclaimed. He was lost in wonder at the mystery of things. (330–31)

The novel is virtually silent about the marriage of Isabel and Gilbert and their first two years together; all that occurs between chapters 35 and 36. Our first information indicates that the marriage is, by now at least, not a happy one. If Isabel represents Gilbert Osmond, as Ralph perceives, the role does not please her. Some compensation results from her involvement in the life of Osmond's daughter, Pansy. She would like to foster the little love affair between her old friend Ned Rosier and Pansy, but Osmond and Serena both in turn discourage Ned. Their choice for Pansy is Lord Warburton, who is back on the scene and showing some interest in the Osmond household—which Isabel properly mistrusts as simply a deflection of his interest in *her* onto the girl. Yet she can offer Ned no encouragement and Warburton no discouragement lest she displease her husband. Isabel is also plagued by the notion that Serena somehow manipulated her into marriage with Osmond, a notion planted in her mind by Mrs. Touchett. Certainly such an idea conflicts with Isabel's still-cherished belief in her own independence and freedom of choice—that she had "acted with her eyes open . . . a free agent; she had looked and considered and chosen" (340). To aggravate that plaguing notion of Serena's manipulation, Isabel is faintly bothered by the vague suspicion that Madame Merle has been somehow involved with Osmond.

That suspicion is encouraged by three events that lead up to and prepare us for the important chapter 42, in which Isabel reviews her life with Osmond and what has brought it about. On returning from a drive into the Campagna she comes upon Madame Merle and Osmond in the drawing room and receives "an impression": they are silent, it is "a familiar silence," and Isabel notices that Osmond is seated although Serena is standing: "there was an anomaly in this that arrested her . . . they were musing, face to face, with the freedom of old friends. . . . But the thing made an image, . . . like a sudden flicker of light. Their relative positions, their absorbed mutual gaze, struck her as something detected" (342–43). Osmond withdraws, Serena engages Isabel in conversation about Rosier and Pansy and then about Warburton and Pansy, which ends with Serena's confessing that she wants to see Pansy married to Lord Warburton—and indicating that she believes Isabel can effect this result:

> "he'll ask her. Especially," said Madame Merle in a moment, "if you make him."
> "If I make him?"
> "It's quite in your power. You've great influence with him."
> (346–47)

At the end of the next chapter (41) Isabel finds herself in the same conversation with Osmond; he also claims that she can bring about the marriage of his daughter and Lord Warburton: "'You must have a great deal of influence with him,' Osmond went on at last. 'The moment you really wish it you can bring him to the point'" (354). He leaves.

She remains seated, alone by the fire, thinking: "The suggestion from another that she had a definite influence on Lord Warburton—that had given her the start that accompanies recognition" (354). Furthermore, "her soul was haunted with terrors," and they were set "into livelier motion . . . [by] the strange impression she had received in the afternoon of her husband's being in more direct communication with Madame Merle than she suspected" (355). The importance of that impression is emphasized at the end of chapter 42 with Isabel "gazing at a remembered vision—that of her husband and Madame Merle unconsciously and familiarly associated" (364).

The recognition that Isabel achieves includes the sense of evil that is embodied in Osmond, a review of his principal characteristics and her mistaken interpretation of them, and a realization of her reasons for marrying him. The terms in which this recognition is expressed are moving and also signally instructive in their rehearsal and echo of terms used in other parts of the novel. She admits her own errors in forming her relationship with Osmond and attempts to measure the extent of her own guilt—not always successfully. She acknowledges some deception of Osmond on her part: "if she had not deceived him in intention she understood how completely she must have done so in fact" (357). And then on the question of Osmond's initially deceiving her, she accepts much of the responsibility for that too: "she had seen only half his nature then . . . now—she saw the whole man. She had . . . mistaken a part for the whole" (357). She argues that it had not been active deception on Osmond's part: she had allowed herself to misjudge the surface presented to her, much as the facade of Osmond's villa in Florence would permit self-deception (see 195).

Just so, architectural imagery functions effectively here to express Isabel's dilemma. In turn, that imagery has numerous further associations. The strongest feature in the list is darkness, suggesting death: "it was as if Osmond deliberately, almost malignantly, had put the lights out one by one" (356): "she had taken the measure of her dwelling. . . . It was the house of darkness, the house of dumbness, the house of suffocation. Osmond's beautiful mind gave it neither light nor air; Osmond's beautiful mind indeed seemed to peep down from a small high window and mock at her" (360). Wonderfully, the images of Isabel's expressive metaphor for her bleak marriage reflect on the actual house she shares with Osmond—"a high house in the very heart of Rome, a dark and massive looking structure . . . the Palazzo Roccanera" (307), Blackrock Castle. If, amidst all this dark imagery, we remember that Osmond is more than once referred to as a prince— Madame Merle early describes him to Isabel as "rather like a demoralised prince in exile" (210) and Ralph soon adds to this depiction by suggesting that "he may be a prince in disguise" (214)—we may then feel urged to call him the Prince of Darkness. That identification is more specifically encouraged by a simple but richly ambivalent comment by his sister, the Countess Gemini: "he has always appeared to believe that he's descended from the gods" (233). This Prince of Darkness, who envied the Pope of Rome, indeed lives in a high house in the very heart of Rome, and consigns his daughter to the keeping of a convent.

There are certainly gripping connections in all this, and quite enough to lead us seriously astray if we are not careful. It might be tempting to "discover" here evidence of a strong anti-Roman Catholic bias in James; but he has anticipated us in that and carefully forestalled that misinterpretation. We must recall that Osmond's envy of the Pope is misguided—"for the consideration he enjoys"—and recognize that it is *he* who makes of the convent a virtual prison to impress the lesson of obedience on Pansy. It is his considered decision to institutionalize Pansy so that she can ponder her failure to capture Warburton, despite Sister Catherine's resonant observation about the girl's situation, "We think it's enough" (463)—as one says of a defeated adversary "He's had enough." It is not the institution itself so much as the abuse that can be made of it. (It must be admitted, however, that James shared the antipathy against religious institutions, and especially highly ritualized ones, to be found in the Protestant tradition of Milton and Blake—one remembers those "Priests in black gowns . . . walking their rounds" in "The Garden of Love"—and of Emerson and his father and Swedenborg.) The crowning touch in Isabel's depiction of Osmond as the Prince of Darkness is added as she thinks of his taking "himself so seriously; it was something appalling"; that leads her to this keen perception: "Under all his culture, his cleverness, his amenity, under his good-nature, his facility, his knowledge of life, his egotism lay hidden like *a serpent in a bank of flowers.*" (360, my italics). The satanic image is surely inescapable.

A further step in Isabel's journey toward understanding seems even more meaningful in its relation to this imagery of darkness, of the satanic. She sees the intended charity of her approach to Osmond as having been something almost desperate—or she half-perceives it as such. The full value of this partial recognition depends on our recalling Isabel's answer to Warburton, as she rejects his proposal of marriage, "It's not what I ask; it's what I can give" (99); her explaining to Mrs. Touchett, "I care very much for money, and that's why I wish Mr. Osmond to have a little" (283); and finally her passionate announcement to Ralph shortly before her marriage: "There have been moments when I would like to go and kneel down by your father's grave: he did perhaps a better thing than he knew when he put it into my power to marry a poor man—a man who has borne his poverty with such dignity, with such indifference. Mr. Osmond . . . has cared for no worldly prize" (293). Now, "poor human-hearted Isabel" looks back at herself:

> She had loved him, she had so anxiously and so ardently given herself [original: "And she loved him"]—a good deal for what she found in him, but a good deal also for what she brought him and what might enrich the gift. . . . But for her money, as she saw today, she would never have done it. And then her mind wandered off to poor Mr. Touchett, sleeping under English turf, the beneficent author of infinite woe! For this was the fantastic fact. At bottom her money had been a burden, had been on her mind, which was

filled with the desire to transfer the weight of it to some other conscience, to some more prepared receptacle. (358)

The useful equation made by the unprepared Isabel now reechoes in
baleful tones: "A large fortune means freedom, and I'm afraid of that"
(193). She has, she now sees, given up that freedom to the "conscience" of the Prince of Darkness, whose egotism lay hidden like the
serpent in the Garden: those are virtually the terms provided by the
novel. Perhaps, given all the conditions, she was bound to do so.

Another of the conditions, particularly important for the main
concerns of the novel, is Isabel's error regarding Osmond's attitude to
the world—"this base ignoble world," she calls it (360). She lines up
her fond expectations and what she has actually realized in opposing
columns: "Instead of leading to the high places of happiness, from
which the world would seem to lie below one, so that one could look
down with a sense of exaltation and advantage, and judge and choose
and pity, it [the "infinite vista of a multiplied life" she had hoped for]
led rather downward and earthward, into realms of restriction and
depression where the sound of other lives, easier and freer, was heard
as from above, and where it served to deepen the feeling of failure"
(356). She recalls that Osmond—the finest and subtlest manly organism she had ever known (358)—"had told her he loved the conventional, but there was a sense in which this seemed a noble declaration
. . . of the love of harmony and order and decency" (359). She recognizes the need for a fresh interpretation of those qualities that had
prompted her to marry him—especially his apparent scorn of the mere
worldly: "he pointed out to her so much of the baseness and shabbi-
ness of life . . . the infinite vulgarity of things and [the necessity] of
keeping oneself unspotted by it. But this base ignoble world, it appeared, was after all what one was to live for; one was to keep it
forever in one's eye, in order not to enlighten or convert or redeem it,
but to extract from it some recognition of one's own superiority" (360).

In a word, her error was in assuming that marriage with Osmond
would be free of the "oppressive . . . narrowing elements" (101) that
Warburton's proposal threatened, all the gross, bare, assertive qualities
that Goodwood's proposal promised. Furthermore, all those coarser,

blatant features of such a union—which marriage to the fine and subtle "manly organism" she conceived Osmond to be would protect her from—seemed to cluster around the baldly sexual presence of both Warburton and (even more obviously) Caspar Goodwood; those she would avoid in her union with Osmond. Evidently her expectations in this respect were initially realized. Isabel recalls fondly "the first year of their life together, so admirably intimate at first" (356; originally just "the first year of their marriage"), and also Osmond as "a man so accomplished and a husband originally at least so tender" (362; originally only "a husband").

That sweet aspect of her marriage—the sexual—soon enough turned, however, to be otherwise aggressive, narrowing, and disgusting, to be, in fact, "hideously unclean": "She was not a daughter of the Puritans, but for all that she believed in such a thing as chastity and even as decency [originally, "such a thing as purity"]. It would appear that Osmond was far from doing anything of the sort, some of his traditions made her push back her skirts. Did all women have lovers? Did they all lie and even the best have their price?" (362). The implications here are somewhat ambiguous: does Isabel allude to his expectation that she enter a liaison with Warburton as part of her exercising her "influence" on Pansy's behalf, or does she suspect (she does not yet know) something of Osmond's adulterous liaisons? Perhaps both are at issue.

Isabel confronts the obvious question and its consequent revelations throughout her vigil by the fire:

> She asked herself if she had married on a fictitious theory. (358) . . .
> She was to think of him . . . as the first gentleman in Europe . . . and that indeed was the reason she had married him. But . . . there was more in the bond than she had meant to put her name to. (360) . . .
> They were strangely married at all events, and it was a horrible life. (363)

She is led, inevitably, to think of Ralph, and in terms that conclude the specific contrast we have looked at earlier. She is on the brink of despair, looking into the pit of "darkness visible" (as Milton described the atmosphere of Hell), but "Ralph's little visit was a lamp in the darkness. . . . It didn't make Gilbert look better to sit for an hour with Ralph. . . . It was simply that Ralph was generous and her husband was not" (363). These thoughts of Ralph—"He made her feel the good of the world" (364)—involve another memory, his extended plea (in chapter 24) against her decision to marry Osmond. The terms of this memory again echo earlier passages containing reference to the sweet airs of gardens: "It lived before her again—it had never had time to die—that morning in the garden at Florence when he had warned her against Osmond. She had only to close her eyes to see the place, to hear his voice, to feel the warm sweet air" (364). That echo will sound again. But her vigil ends.

At this point we are left wondering what such a profound and extensive recognition of her situation will prompt Isabel to do: where will she turn, what help is there, what further revelations remain to be given her?

5

Revelation, Action, Recovery

REVELATION AND ACTION

One result of Isabel's soul-searching vigil, portrayed in chapter 42, is the reawakening of her old sense of self-reliance and independent-mindedness. While being careful to avoid a direct confrontation in which she will be obliged to act in defiance of her husband's wishes, Isabel now begins to free herself from the position of complete submission to those wishes.

She had told the hopeful Ned Rosier that although she favored him as Pansy's suitor, she could do nothing on his behalf—nothing, that is, to sway Osmond to accept him as a future son-in-law: "It's not that I won't; I simply can't!" (317). As chapter 43 moves to its close, Rosier laments his plight to Isabel: he correctly sees Lord Warburton as his competitor and fears Isabel may have shifted her favor to that suitor. She responds with a realistic mixture of boldness and caution: "I'll do what I can for you. I'm afraid it won't be much, but what I can I'll do" (373).

Isabel's response is cautiously bold, not because her favoring Rosier is by itself such a strong move but because it implicitly opposes

Osmond's (and Madame Merle's) favoring Warburton. Isabel's problem with Warburton as suitor for Pansy is complex but not unduly complicated. First, she believes that Pansy loves Rosier and does not love Warburton. Second, she is impressed by the argument of Gilbert and Serena that she has "influence" with Warburton, in short, that she can use his evidently continuing love for her to persuade him to marry Pansy—the exact wielding of that influence and bestowing of the consequent reward upon Warburton to be left up to Isabel. Third, Isabel is not blind to the material advantages Pansy would enjoy as Warburton's wife. Finally, Isabel still does not wish to defy Osmond directly and blatantly, so long as this can be avoided.

She manages to attack the second question in a conversation with Ralph, Warburton's close friend. She asks, "But is he really in love?" Ralph replies, "Very much, I think. I can make that out." Then, to try to straighten out the matter of who is the actual subject in question, Isabel resumes:

> "I thought you knew. Lord Warburton tells me he wants, of all things in the world, to marry Pansy. . . . Is it your belief that he really cares for her?"
> "Ah, for Pansy, no!" cried Ralph positively.
> "But you said just now he did."
> Ralph waited a moment. "That he cared for you, Mrs. Osmond."
> (387)

Isabel rejects this and continues to ask for confirmation of Warburton's caring for Pansy. She does not get it, and so bursts out passionately, "Ah, Ralph, you give me no help!" We readily understand her passionate exasperation, but James adds a poignant observation that makes the outburst otherwise meaningful—and, at last, memorable: "It was the first time she had alluded to the need for help, and the words shook her cousin with their violence . . . it seemed to him that at last the gulf between them had been bridged" (388).

Isabel must then turn to Pansy to discover whether it would be proper to continue in her promise to do what she can for Rosier and to continue to discourage Warburton. "What Isabel wished to do was to hear from her [Pansy's] own lips that her mind was not occupied with Lord Warburton; . . . if Pansy should display the smallest germ of a disposition to encourage Lord Warburton her own duty was to hold her tongue" (390–91). Even if Pansy's disposition is what Isabel expects it to be (as of course it is) she must be careful not to appear to the girl to be acting in opposition to Osmond's wishes by expressing open defiance of his will. Isabel's care in this matter to seem not to be taking sides either way succeeds—although she feels "hideously insincere" (392)—in that Pansy is led to the point of freely acknowledging Warburton's understanding of the situation: "He knows I don't want to marry, and he wants me to know that he therefore won't trouble me. . . . That is all we've said to each other. And he doesn't care for me either. Ah no, there's no danger" (394). Isabel sustains her position to the end: "'You must tell your father that,' she remarked reservedly."

The abrupt, impatient response to Isabel's careful behavior here may be exasperation, but Warburton's next appearance on the scene argues that she has succeeded without initiating belligerent confrontation. He has come simply to say goodbye to Isabel and to Pansy. A brief exchange between him and Isabel confirms Pansy's account of their understanding. He says,

> "I want very much to see her."
> "I'm glad it's the last time," said Isabel.
> "So am I. She doesn't care for me."
> "No, she doesn't care for you." (399)

And he leaves. As Isabel has been blunt and dispassionate with Warburton, so has she avoided an act of defiance against Osmond.

The result, however, is severe anger and recrimination on Osmond's part. *He* is defiant and so exposes further his ill-nature and his selfishness in his attack on Isabel. He accuses her not simply of failing to achieve the ends he sought but of actually working to thwart him (402–403). If the reader's exasperation reasserts itself here—"See! What good did it do Isabel to avoid taking sides, confronting Osmond, showing defiance?"—it should be calmed by recognition of the novel's developing the idea that Isabel's just restraint has provoked Osmond to further identify himself with the evil that has him in its grip. If she is not yet ready for active confrontation in the full confidence of her awakened self-trust and independent-mindedness, she is moving toward it and certainly refusing to be submissive to her husband's wishes.

A further step in that direction leads to her last meeting with Ralph in Rome. He announces his imminent departure for England; she says, "I ought to go with you, you know" (418); and they frankly admit to a real intimacy, in their restrained and gentle way, that is mutually gratifying:

> "You've been my best friend," she said.
> "It was for you that I wanted—that I wanted to live. But I'm of no use to you now."
> Then it came over her more poignantly that . . . she could not part with him that way. "If you should send for me, I'd come," she said at last.
> "Your husband won't consent to that."
> "Oh yes, I can arrange it."
> "I shall keep that for my last pleasure," said Ralph.
> In answer to which she simply kissed him. (419)

The note here of blossoming defiance is only just perceptible; but the reaffirmation of the union between Isabel and her most generous and adoring friend is unmistakable.

There is yet another note in this exchange that further develops the idea of Isabel's recovered self-trust and enlightened self-interest. The emphasis is carefully specified, nicely defined. To Isabel's suggestion that she ought to accompany Ralph to England he sensibly replies that Osmond wouldn't like it; Isabel again asserts herself—though not quite defiantly: "No, he wouldn't like it. But I might go, all the same." When Ralph then half-jocularly observes, "Fancy my being a cause of disagreement between a lady and her husband," Isabel adds, "That's why I don't go" (419). If that were the end of the conversation it might offer some justification for the simplistic claim (still asserted by one kind of reader) that Isabel remains the dutiful, obedient, submissive wife who, if she were to leave Osmond to visit England, would then dutifully and submissively return to him. It is not, however, the end of the conversation; the continuation quite explicitly denies that simplistic interpretation.

> "I'm afraid," said Isabel. . . . "I'm afraid."
> . . . Ralph could not resist so easy an opportunity. "Afraid of your husband?"
> "Afraid of myself!" she said, getting up. . . . "If I were afraid of my husband that would be simply my duty. That's what women are expected to be." (419)

(And there is a memorable statement of the "new woman," who denies the weight of the old traditional demand of wifely duty; it is also typical of James—and of Blake and his other predecessors—in that he saw doing one's duty in the usual sense of that term as cause for neither praise nor blame; the excuse of doing one's duty, in fact, seemed to be an escape from moral choice.)

The thrust of Isabel's careful specification gains strength from being a kind of echo of a slightly earlier affirmation to Henrietta on her asking Isabel why she doesn't just leave Osmond. Part of her response is that she can't change things that way. Henrietta's "I hope you don't mean to say you like him" prompts Isabel's affirmation.

> Isabel debated. "No, I don't like him. I can tell you because I'm weary of my secret. But that's enough; I can't announce it on the housetops."
> Henrietta gave a laugh. "Don't you think you're rather too considerate?"
> "It's not of him that I'm considerate—it's of myself!" Isabel answered. (407)

The emphatic parallel—"Afraid of myself" and "considerate . . . of myself"—establishes the point, which the simple Henrietta and a slightly obtuse reader might miss. Isabel's concern, she asserts, is herself; her sense of duty is duty to herself. This is not narrow, benighted selfishness, not the equivalent of saying simply "I don't care about him." Isabel is yet again affirming the importance of enlightened self-interest, of the self-love that the Judeo-Christian tradition has maintained is the condition requisite for loving one's "neighbors."

Because of all this evidence of the emergence—not exactly reemergence—of Isabel's more mature independence and proper self-concern, the novel arranges to reward her, so to speak. Consequently—and sequence here seems the equivalent of cause and effect—Isabel is vouchsafed two further revelations necessary to the full development of her burgeoning maturity; and they in turn allow her another successful step of progress, of passive (not defiant) triumph.

As chapter 49 opens, Madame Merle resumes the questioning of Isabel that Osmond had earlier instigated regarding what had become of Warburton and his attention to Pansy, "whether Lord Warburton changed his mind of his own movement or because you recommended it. To please himself I mean, or to please you" (429). The seering question has been beautifully set up in the report of Isabel's musings at the opening of the conversation; these musings are a continuation of her night vigil in chapter 42 and indeed of the scene and the expressions of confidence that had preceded it: Madame Merle's and Gilbert Osmond's confidence in her ability to influence Warburton. Isabel recalls "that day when she happened to be struck with the manner in which the wonderful lady and her own husband sat together. . . . a strange truth was filtering into her soul. Madame Merle's interest was identical with Osmond's: that was enough" (428). So, as Madame Merle pursues her interrogation, leading to the reverberating plural pronoun at its end, Isabel is more alert than ever. It leads to the request, the demand, that Isabel relinquish her supposed influence on Lord Warburton: "Let him off—let us have him!" "Us"? Alert but startled, Isabel asks, "Who are you—what are you? . . . What have you to do with my husband?" And then, poignantly, "What have you to do with me?" That last is a crucial question; it is a dramatic moment and

James gives it an exquisite presentation, with each detail a paying piece. Watch Serena:

> Madame Merle slowly got up, stroking her muff, but not removing her eyes from Isabel's face. "Everything!" she answered.
> Isabel sat there looking up at her, without rising; her face was almost a prayer to be enlightened. But the light of this woman's eyes seemed only a darkness. (430)

Darkness visible! A fitting ally for the Prince of Darkness.

Isabel is not yet quite sure. She asks herself, "with an almost childlike horror," whether Serena Merle merits "the great historical epithet of *wicked*" (431). But she has seen; the recognition has been vouchsafed; Isabel need only find the appropriate terms of definition. Assistance in finding those terms constitutes her second "reward," and that comes from the Countess Gemini. She is a rare little bird of a character, but she had taken a liking to Mrs. Osmond when she visited at the Palazzo Roccanera for a week during the first winter of her brother's marriage. Before her second visit with the Osmonds she says a good deal to Henrietta about Gilbert and about the gossip concerning the attention Warburton has been paying to Isabel. Henrietta disabuses her about the gossip but expresses fear that her old friend is unhappy. The Countess responds, "If Isabel's unhappy, I'm very sorry for her, but I can't help it. I might tell her something that would make her worse, but I can't tell her anything that would console her" (380). The Countess then learns at first hand of Isabel's unhappiness—and indeed tells her something: that Pansy is the child of Gilbert Osmond and Serena Merle, that he was Madame Merle's lover "for six or seven years" (451), and that Serena wanted Isabel to become Mrs. Osmond "Because you had money; and because she believed you would be good to Pansy" (543).

Countess Gemini explains that one of the reasons why Serena would not herself marry Gilbert was "the fear that seeing her with Pansy people would put things together—would even see a resemblance. She has had a terror lest the mother should betray herself. . . .

the mother has never done so." "'Yes, yes, the mother has done so,' said Isabel. . . . 'She betrayed herself to me the other day, though I didn't recognise her. There appeared to have been a chance of Pansy's making a great marriage, and in her disappointment at its not coming off she almost dropped her mask'" (454). At last Isabel has to ask the Countess how she knows all this; the Countess, slightly miffed, answers, "Let's assume that I've invented it!" (455).

But Isabel knows better. She has come to the Countess's revelation quite prepared, subconsciously, to hear something very like it: Isabel's ears are ringing with an echo. Chapter 51 has begun with Isabel's informing Osmond that Ralph is dying and that she wishes to go to England to see him. Osmond forbids it. A clear confrontation has arisen: "If you leave Rome to-day it will be a piece of the most deliberate, the most calculated opposition." She replies, "It's your opposition that's calculated. It's quite malignant." Isabel "knew that between them they had arrived at a crisis" (445). In Osmond's defense of his position, he utters loudly and clearly the words that constitute the meaningful echo: "Your cousin's nothing to you; he's nothing to us. You smile most expressively when I talk about *us*, but I assure you that *we, we*, Mrs. Osmond, is all I know . . ." (446). His use of the plural pronoun is surely responsible for Isabel's smiling "most expressively": it is a repetition of Madame Merle's exhortation to Isabel regarding Warburton, "let *us* have him!" (430; my italics). The Countess Gemini has completed Isabel's recognition; she asks pointedly, "Now will you give up your journey?" Isabel replies, most significantly, "Ah, I must see Ralph!" (455). She has at last determined to *act* on her own wishes and specifically in defiance of Osmond's proscription.

Before she acts on that hopefully inspired compulsion Isabel must undergo another confrontation, and it is a signal success. Pansy has been returned to the convent. Osmond's intention is clearly punitive: he wants her to feel the weight of his displeasure at her failure to entice Warburton into a proposal of marriage. Isabel has gone to the convent to visit the girl, and her sense of the place underlines the use Osmond makes of it: "It produced to-day more than before the impression of a well-appointed prison; for it was not possible to pretend Pansy was free to leave it" (456). There she finds Serena Merle, who greets her and prattles on with all the embarrassed volubility of a criminal caught red-handed. Isabel recognizes in all this that Madame Merle realizes that she is caught, that Isabel "knew her secret" (458). The exasperation of the impatient reader at Isabel's reluctance to take sides, to show defiance, to provoke armed confrontation ought to be assuaged here. Her restraint brings its own success and reward: "Isabel saw it all. . . . It might have been a great moment for her, for it might have been a moment of triumph. That Madame Merle had lost her pluck and saw before her the phantom of exposure—this in itself was revenge, this in itself was almost the promise of a brighter day. . . . Isabel enjoyed that knowledge . . . Isabel's only revenge was to be silent still" (458–59).

She then sees Pansy, who declares she has been chastened and in fact is "a little afraid" of Gilbert and Serena: "Oh, I'll do everything they want. Only if you're here I shall do it more easily" (462). Pansy's plight provokes two responses from Isabel: "I won't desert you" (462) and "I'll come back" (463). Madame Merle has remained. She adds the final touch of revelation by reporting that Ralph Touchett was responsible for Isabel's inheritance of £70,000, that although it was Mr. Touchett's money it was Ralph's idea: "He imparted to you that extra lustre which was to make you a brilliant match." "Isabel went to the door and . . . stood a moment with her hand on the latch. Then she said—it was her only revenge: 'I believed it was you I had to thank!'" (464). She then sets off to see Ralph.

ACTION AND REBIRTH

Isabel has committed herself to action, to direct and specific defiance of Osmond. Her journey to England is both a flight to Ralph and an escape from Osmond. We have seen how the series of revelations determined her to renounce her obedience to the Prince of Darkness and seek a safe haven with the cousin she can be sure adores her selflessly. She had thought, some time before Ralph's leaving Rome, of the blessed peace she had known years ago in the innocent flush of her arrival at Gardencourt. "There seemed to Isabel in these days something sacred in Gardencourt; no chapter of the past was more perfectly irrecoverable" (414). This cast of mind returns to her during her flight from Rome: "Gardencourt had been her starting-point, and to those muffled chambers it was at least a temporary solution to return. She had gone forth in her strength; she had come back in her weakness, and if the place had been a rest to her before, it would be a sanctuary now" (465).

The fact of change is clearly enough expressed at the opening of chapter 53, and the terms of expression suggest explicitly enough that the change is a kind of spiritual death for Isabel. Whether or not this "death" is to be followed by rebirth we will have to wait and see, although subtle hints of such a development are present from the beginning of this stage of her career.

> On her journey from Rome her mind had been given up to vagueness; she was unable to question the future. She performed this journey with sightless eyes and took little pleasure in the countries she traversed, decked out though they were in the richest freshness of spring. Her thoughts followed their course through other countries—strange-looking, dimly-lighted, pathless lands, in which there was no change of seasons, but only, as it seemed, a perpetual dreariness of winter. . . . All purpose, all intention, was suspended: all desire too save the single desire to reach her much embracing refuge. (464–65)

The geography of this journey through the "pathless lands" has been more recently adapted and employed by T. S. Eliot for the setting of his characters in *The Waste Land*. And the voices there repeat the anguish of Isabel's condition:

> The voice of the hyacinth girl's swain—
> I could not
> Speak, and my eyes failed, I was neither
> Living nor dead, and I knew nothing . . .

—and then the voice of the thunder—
Prison and palace and reverberation
Of thunder of spring over distant mountains
He who was living is now dead
We who were living are now dying
With a little patience

The conditional optimism of Eliot's great poem urges the spiritual death of the "old man" that it may lead to rebirth: in both James's novel and Eliot's poem spring is "there"—and may be realized and enjoyed when the right conditions are fulfilled. Perhaps Isabel's situation is even more hopeful.

> She envied Ralph his dying, for if one were thinking of rest that was the most perfect of all. To cease utterly, to give it all up and not know anything more—this idea was as sweet as the vision of a cool bath in a marble tank, in a darkened chamber, in a hot land.
> She had moments indeed in her journey from Rome which were almost as good as being dead. (465)

This is of course not the end, for it is quite clearly a transitional moment: before "the grey curtain of her indifference closed her in," "She saw herself, in the distant years, still in the attitude of a woman who had her life to live, and these intimations contradicted the spirit of the present hour." And finally, "Deep in her soul—deeper than any appetite for renunciation—was the sense that life would be her business for a long time to come. And at moments there was something inspiring, almost enlivening, in the conviction. It was a proof of strength—it was a proof she should some day be happy again" (466). Momentarily, indifference intervenes; it has replaced the wish for death, and perhaps tokens a change of direction—to rebirth. That will depend. . . .

Down at Gardencourt the note of change is sounded again—"to the servants Mrs. Osmond was a stranger" (471)—but the way down has not yet definitely become the way up. She is greeted by Mrs. Touchett and brought up to date on Ralph's illness. Isabel is able to see Ralph, but an interval must pass before they can actually converse together: "he was unable to speak; . . . for he lay three days in a kind of grateful silence. . . . Ralph, however, spoke at last—on the evening of the third day" (476). Then the words spill out, and the profound spiritual love they share is allowed to manifest itself frankly. Certain details of their intercourse stand out. She wishes she could be his Alcestis:

> "O Ralph, you've been everything! . . . I would die if you could live. But I don't wish you to live; I would die myself not to lose you."
> "You won't lose me—you'll keep me. Keep me in your heart; I shall be nearer to you than I've ever been. Dear Isabel, life is better; for in life there's love. Death is good—but there's no love." (477)

Ralph confesses that he was indeed responsible for her inherited riches and thus for her marriage to Osmond; he laments, "I believe I ruined you," and again, "You were ground in the very mill of the conventional" (478). Isabel admits that she thought Ralph had always understood her plight as Mrs. Osmond: "I didn't like it. But now I like it" (478). Then he raises the question of whether she will return to Osmond; Isabel doesn't know. They would both like her to remain at Gardencourt: "For me you'll always be here," says Isabel. Then Ralph's closing observation—"I don't believe that such a generous mistake as yours can hurt you for more than a little"—leads to his reaffirmation of enduring love, a complement to his adjuration, "Keep me in your heart": "'And remember this,' he continued, 'that if you've been hated, you've also been loved. Ah but, Isabel—*adored!*' he just audibly and lingeringly breathed" (479; the original stops with "loved").

The final chapter opens with the account of the fulfillment of Ralph's prophecy regarding the ghost of Gardencourt. It is a simple enough matter: Isabel retires, not expecting Ralph to "last out the night," and apparently sees the ghost as he had predicted, "the first night she ever spent at Gardencourt, that if she should live to suffer enough she might someday see the ghost. . . . She apparently had fulfilled the necessary condition . . ." (479). What disturbs the apparent simplicity is James's peculiar manipulation of language in his account of the visitation, for it produces a rather arresting ambiguity. Pronouns refer clearly enough, it seems, to Ralph, yet they are accompanied by *an appositive reference to the ghost:*

> in the cold, faint dawn, she knew that a spirit was standing by her bed. She had believed that as the night wore on she should hear a knock at her door. She heard no knock, but at the time the darkness began vaguely to grow grey she started up from her pillow as abruptly as if she had received a summons. It seemed to her for an instant that he was standing there—a vague hovering figure in the vagueness of the room. She stared a moment; she saw his white face—his kind eyes; then she saw there was nothing. She was not afraid; she was only sure. (479)

Is Ralph then the ghost of Gardencourt? Is this ghost similar to the ghosts of *The Turn of the Screw?* Perhaps. But if not, one might ponder its significance.

After the funeral, the two former suitors of Isabel Archer pay their respects to Mrs. Osmond, rather as though she were still Isabel Archer. Lord Warburton then leaves graciously enough. Goodwood is much more insistent and will not bid her goodbye, but pursues her into London. There, however, he learns from Henrietta that Isabel has gone: "this morning she started for Rome" (490).

What everyone asks of this ending is "Why?!! Why doesn't she just leave Osmond?" The possible reasons are all there in the novel. To begin with, she has promised Pansy that she will return; she certainly has—we've seen that. Then, she wants to get away from the persistent and threateningly phallic Caspar; she tells him flatly that she is going back to Rome "To get away from *you!*" (488)—which seems rather unambiguous. Furthermore, she feels it necessary to do her duty as a responsible and obedient wife, and with that she must respect her marriage vows; that dual reason demands her attention repeatedly—and if we aren't especially persuaded by the demands of the sacrament of marriage we might at least feel that she ought to keep her word and do her duty (although we might also feel that we've been through this one already).

Yet the novel also gives us the means to discount or cancel all these "reasons," as, indeed, Isabel herself does with varying degrees of explicitness. The decision is first anticipated by Henrietta's boldly asking (understandably: she's just like us!), "Why don't you leave him?" Isabel's answers to this and to Henrietta's repetition of the question demand close attention.

> "I can't change that way," Isabel said.
> "Why not I should like to know? You won't confess that you've made a mistake. You're too proud." . . .
> ". . . One must accept one's deeds. I married him before all the world. . . . One can't change that way," Isabel repeated. (407)

That may not seem tremendously helpful, but it is worth noting that Isabel does *not* say that she (or "One") can't change, but rather that she (or "One") can't change *that way;* the implication clearly is that she has in mind *other* ways. (And we might also observe that James does not offer this explanation as being peculiarly Isabel's, but as an explanation of general applicability—not just "*I* can't" but the indefinite or general "*One* can't"—as though he were offering a universal principle.)

The matter of her promise to Pansy is managed similarly. Henrietta meets Isabel on her return to England and observes that her breaking away "must have been hellish" (originally "awful"); "Isabel didn't deny that it had been hellish" (469; originally "awful"!). Henrietta continues, "I don't see why you promised little Miss Osmond to go back."

> "I'm not sure I myself see now," Isabel replied. "But I did then."
> "If you've forgotten your reason perhaps you won't return."
> Isabel waited a moment. "Perhaps I shall find another." (469)

That there may be another way of changing than by leaving Osmond, that there may be another reason for returning than the promise made to Pansy—that double-barreled possibility ought to pique our curiosity and interest. If not those, what then?

Revelation, Action, Recovery

Caspar Goodwood's final attempt to win Isabel has, however, provided the most serious difficulty in understanding Isabel's ultimate decision, and it just may be the toughest bone of contention among critics of *The Portrait of a Lady*. There is at least no mistaking James's intention for the 1881 version as (we have no reason to doubt) for the revision as well. His own notes read: "Isabel's return to London, and interview with Caspar G.—His passionate outbreak; he beseeches her to return with him to America. She is greatly moved, she feels the full force of his devotion—to which she has never done justice; but she refuses. She starts again for Italy—and her departure is the climax and termination of the story" (*Notebooks*, 15).

We have to remind ourselves—or, rather, be alert to the means James uses in the novel to remind us—of how Isabel has responded during the novel to the overtures of Caspar and indeed to those of Lord Warburton and of Gilbert Osmond and even of Ralph Touchett. Isabel was sensitive, at some level of her consciousness, to the sexual, the specifically phallic, quality of the proposals of Goodwood and Warburton when she rejected them and opted instead for the far more suave and understated offer—apparently free of the frankly physical and blatantly gross elements it might have manifested—of Osmond ("The finest—in the sense of being the subtlest—manly organism she had ever known" [358; originally, "The finest individual she had ever known"!]), who then proved to be a "tender" husband, at least at first during the "admirably intimate" time of her marriage. Finally, her first long moment of recognition of this matter (and others), in the vigil of chapter 42, ends with her renewed contrasting of Osmond and Ralph: her cousin loved her generously and selflessly (as she would now translate the "light" of Ralph's visit, his making her feel the good of the world) with a love that involved no sexual bargain—suave or aggressive—whatsoever. Now he is dead. Warburton has said his last good-bye. Osmond she has left in Rome. Caspar alone remains to be dealt with, as she always knew he would.

Early in the novel, following Warburton's hunting crop proposal, Isabel's thoughts turn to her American suitor: "Sometimes Caspar Goodwood had seemed to range himself on the side of her destiny, to be the stubbornest fact she knew; she said to herself at such times that she might evade him for a time, but that she must make terms with him at last—terms which would be certain to be favourable to himself" (105). Ralph's stirring Emersonian exhortation to her to live as she likes best, to spread her wings and rise, and her subsequent confession of fear at the inheritance of the large fortune (which meant freedom) have yet made Isabel ponder her destiny once again. Inevitably, it seems, that involves Caspar Goodwood, who when all else is gone will remain. "But she reflected that she herself might know the humiliation of change, might really, for that matter, come to the end of things that were not Caspar (even though there appeared so many of them), and find rest in those very elements of his presence which struck her now as impediments to the finer respiration. It was conceivable that these impediments should some day prove a sort of blessing in disguise—a clear and quiet harbour enclosed by a brave granite breakwater" (194). (The terms used to describe that conceivable blessing—the marine imagery of harbor and breakwater—find their echo in the closing passages of the novel.)

After Isabel's momentous vigil in chapter 42, Henrietta has had her informative interview with the Countess Gemini and in turn enlightened Caspar regarding Isabel's unhappiness. He comes to Rome, wanting to intercede. Henrietta informs Isabel of his arrival. She thinks of her last meeting with him as having had "quite the character of a complete rupture" (404), and the terms of her recollection create a flood of marine imagery. She feels a touch of guilt, or at least responsibility, for Caspar "represented the only serious harm that (to her belief) she had ever done in the world: he was the only person with an unsatisfied claim on her. She had made him unhappy, she couldn't help it; and his unhappiness was a grim reality" (404). Caspar succeeds in securing an interview with Isabel, in Rome, just before he is to leave to accompany the ailing Ralph back to England. The interview crackles with passion and distinctly anticipates the final scene between them at the end of the novel, and *that* scene refers quite specifically to this one in Rome. He has drawn her away from the social crowd to an adjoining room. "She had for him the same familiar grace. She seemed to wait for him to speak. Now that he was alone with her all the passion he had never stifled surged into his senses; it hummed in his eyes and made things swim around him. The bright empty room grew dim and blurred, and through the heaving veil he felt her hover before him with gleaming eyes and parted lips. If he had seen her more distinctly he would have perceived her smile was fixed and a trifle forced—that she was frightened at what she saw in his own face" (425). There again is the marine imagery—passion "surged" and "made things swim"; and there is in Isabel's "gleaming eyes and parted lips" at least the glimmer of passionate response. The fixed, forced smile indicates an attempt to mask and control her feelings—of fright, certainly, and of something more.

At the close of the novel Caspar returns, demanding that Isabel "make terms" with him, certainly expressing passionate desire, and perhaps presenting himself as a blessing in disguise. Claiming that Ralph had at the last commissioned him to look after her, Caspar offers to save her from her wretched marriage by carrying her off under his care to America. The passage recalls their last, passion-filled meeting in Rome: "Goodwood spoke very fast; he was as excited as when they had parted in Rome. Isabel had hoped that condition would subside" (486). She experiences "a feeling of danger" (486). Caspar offers, first, sympathetic understanding and support: "you're afraid to go back. You're perfectly alone; you don't know where to turn. . . . I want you to think of me" (488). She certainly appears to be alone; she has evidently not yet decided "where to turn," although she *has* left the "temporary solution" that Gardencourt afforded. "Why should you go back," he pursues, repeating Henrietta's earlier challenge; "why should you go through that ghastly form?" (That final word inevitably recalls—to us as to Isabel—the fiercely formal Osmond.) Caspar resumes that tack, next, as though he had been privy to Isabel's thoughts during her nocturnal soul-searching in chapter 42: "You must save what you can of your life; . . . It would be an insult to you to assume that you care for the look of things, for what people will say, for the *bottomless idiocy of the world*" (488; my italics). He insists on their freedom, the absence of responsibility, the vastness of opportunity that is open to them: "We can do absolutely as we please;

to whom under the sun do we owe anything? . . . The world's all before us—and the world's very big" (489). (We have to pause a moment
to note that Caspar's large claim repeats the language of the concluding lines of Milton's *Paradise Lost*, the end of the account of the fall—
the *fortunate* fall it is sometimes called—of "our Grand Parents"
Adam and Eve:

> Som natural tears they drop't, but wip'd them soon;
> The World was all before them, where to choose
> Thir place of rest, and Providence thir guide:
> They hand in hand with wand'ring steps and slow,
> Through *Eden* took thir solitarie way.

James's point in employing the Miltonic language we must ponder
when we return to the question later.)

Isabel's response to Caspar is, "The world's very small"; James
quickly adds, "but it was not what she meant," as though to suggest
the ambivalence inherent in her attitude. We cannot, however, escape
her urgent sense of gratitude at the offer: "The world in truth had
never seemed so large; it seemed to open out, all round her, to take
the form of a mighty sea, where she floated in fathomless waters. She
had wanted help, and here was help; it had come in a rushing torrent"
(488). The imagery of the sea must recall to us her earlier conception
of Goodwood as a potential blessing in disguise, a clear and quiet and
protected harbor (194). Her gratitude for his offer of help shines
through the attendant feeling of danger. "She couldn't have told you
whether it was because she was afraid, or because such a voice in the
darkness seemed of necessity a boon; but she listened to him as she
had never listened before; his words dropped into her soul. They produced a sort of stillness in all her being . . ." (487). Let there be no
confusion, then, over the fact that Goodwood's offer touches Isabel
distinctly and exerts a definite appeal—at least for the moment.

But certain elements of Caspar's argument in support of his offer
to take care of her are a repetition of items that Isabel has previously
confronted, and she—or at least the thrust of the novel—has already

dismissed them. And unless she has gone back on herself, these items are to be confronted and likewise dismissed again. First, her early response to Henrietta's "Why don't you leave him?" is quite as apt now: "I [One] can't change that way." And that response now carries with it the strength of her similar answer to Henrietta's comment on the promise to return to Pansy—"if you've forgotten your reason"—"Perhaps I shall find another." Second, in inviting Isabel's defiance of the world, Goodwood is repeating Osmond's deceptive stance, though with a slight difference; both suggest the possibility of disregarding the world and fail to recognize that in spite of everything the world remains *there*, of necessity. Furthermore, Isabel has already demonstrated her intention of avoiding commitment to either end of the polarity between defiance and submission, of seeking what viable compromise there may be. Third, the promise of the boundless opportunities, the limitless freedom of the "very big" world has been carefully defined as a delusion. After her year of travel, of seeing the world and, in consequence, feeling exhilaratingly superior to her sister Lily Ludlow and family, Isabel's self-congratulatory exuberance is expressed in language that specifically anticipates Goodwood's excited rhetoric. Isabel's attitude was "The world lay before her—she could do whatever she chose. There was a deep thrill in it all" (273). Nevertheless, those reasons seem again to exert their appeal to Isabel—at least for the moment.

There is, however, one other dramatic, gripping, and evidently puzzling feature of Goodwood's appeal—its blatantly sexual quality. The evidence would seem unmistakable that she is attracted rather than repulsed by this feature. Recalling the sexual history (so to speak) of Isabel's career—especially the "admirable intimacy" of the first year of her marriage, long since withdrawn—surely makes such an attraction understandable. Her initial response inaugurates that recall: replying to Goodwood's question as to why she plans to return to Rome, Isabel exclaims, "To get away from *you!*" Then, James explains,

> But this expressed only a little of what she felt. The rest was that she had never been loved before. She had believed it, but this was

71

different, this was the hot wind of the desert, at the approach of which the others dropped dead, like mere sweet airs of the garden. It wrapped her about; it lifted her off her feet, while the very taste of it, as something potent, acrid and strange, forced open her set teeth. (488)

The third sentence of this passage—containing the metaphor of the "hot wind" and the "sweet airs"—was added in the 1908 version of the novel (as was, in fact, the last two-thirds of the concluding sentence, from "while the very taste of it" to the "set teeth"). That revision matches an earlier one of the same kind near the end of chapter 12, in Warburton's marriage proposal to Isabel. It was noted in chapter 3 of this study that James replaced a rather vague and abstract passage with one of concrete and specific imagery; the imagery of that replacement now becomes signally important: "the fragrance straight in her face . . . of she knew not what strange gardens, what charged airs" (100). Both revisions were calculated to create a network of imagery and thus to strengthen the expression of a particular theme by linking up with two other important passages in the novel. These other passages, retained untouched from the 1881 version, use exactly this imagery. In chapter 31 Isabel awaits a visit from Goodwood: "The tall window was open, and though its green shutters were partly drawn the bright air of the garden had come in through a broad interstice and filled the room with warmth and perfume" (270). In chapter 42 she is thinking of Ralph and recalls his warning her against Osmond in chapter 34: "It lived before her again . . . that morning in the garden at Florence. . . . She had only to close her eyes to see the place, to hear his voice, to feel the warm sweet air" (364). The network of imagery draws together the quality of Warburton's proposal, the atmosphere of Caspar's visit in Florence, and of Ralph's visit there as well, and thus creates a steadily sustained theme. The quality of this final scene between Isabel and Caspar, which completes the thematic statement by means of a startling contrast, is consequently enhanced and the special significance of Caspar's final appeal given particular emphasis. All those earlier mild airs, fragrant with garden-variety innocence—

even allowing for the piquant phallic quality in the cases of Warburton and Goodwood—pale impressively by contrast with this final scene with its hot, acrid wind that forced open her set teeth and lifted her off her feet.

The next step toward the emotional climax of the scene sustains the note of Isabel's passionate abandon, or rather the note of her *desire for* passionate abandon; for the marine imagery here can be deceptive. During this passage we see Isabel's struggle and the direction in which it is leading her. At first Goodwood's offer of help sweeps over her like a torrent—perhaps slaking the yearning thirst that has been aggravated by the "hot wind of the desert": "she believed just then that to let him take her in his arms would be the next best thing to her dying. This belief, for a moment, was a kind of rapture, in which she let herself sink and sink. In the movement she seemed to beat with her feet, in order to catch herself, to feel something to rest on" (489). The sense of surrender and abandonment is obvious enough, and even of orgasmic ecstasy ("the next best thing to her dying"). But that sense lasts only "for a moment," and within that moment she ceases to seek the welcome bath of the passionate torrent and seeks instead some solid support to prevent her from sinking deep into that rapturous medium. We have to make an important distinction here about Isabel's quite persistent apprehensiveness: it is not now the fear of passionate rapture itself so much as the fear of *succumbing* to it—of *losing herself* gratefully in it as she yields submissively to her need for sexual gratification—that concerns her. *Giving herself up* is the threatening temptation.

There is another consideration as well: the phrase "the next best thing to her dying" distinctly echoes fragments of the account at the beginning of chapter 53 of Isabel's almost desperate journey from Rome. Then she had "envied Ralph his dying"; the idea that "to cease utterly, to give it all up . . . was as sweet as the vision of a cool bath in a marble tank, in a darkened chamber, in a hot land" (465). But that envy and that sweet vision are then followed by the lucid sense that life would be her business still and that she would be happy again, by her colloquy with Henrietta over the promise to Pansy, and by the inspirational interview with Ralph and his reiteration of his love for her. She is once again, however, in that "hot land" and feeling the "hot wind of the desert" and desiring the relief of a torrent or a cool bath. Will she now give up, after all? How much more can she stand?

There remains the culminating kiss. That is richly revised from the laconic blandness of the 1881 version: "His kiss was like white lightning; when it was dark again she was free." In James's revision the explicitly phallic quality of the embrace is inescapable; we must pay close attention to the tenses of the verbs: "His kiss was like white lightning, a flash that spread, and spread again, and stayed; and it was extraordinarily as if, while she took it, she felt each thing in his hard manhood that *had* least *pleased* her, each aggressive fact of his face, his figure, his presence, justified of its intense identity and made one with this act of possession" (489; my italics). The last word of the quotation says a great deal (D. H. Lawrence would have understood and sympathized fully with Isabel): to yield to her own urgent desire would be to risk giving herself up, relinquishing self-reliance, abdicating from her newly won position of independence. She realizes, in that passionate moment, that she may be almost beyond her depth (as swimmers say) and she almost misses something to rest on as she is about to sink: "So she had heard of those wrecked and under water following a train of images before they sink. But when darkness came she was free" (489).

Free? If so, to ask it again, why does she return to Rome? Surely the answer must be—in spite of all—that she feels she must do her duty, that she must remain faithful to her marriage vows. Throughout the unhappy years under Osmond's rule Isabel has looked again and again at those traditionally binding vows. Furthermore, she has also pondered the weight of her responsibility for decisions taken in ignorance or partial ignorance, and also for decisions taken under the undue influence of others. These preoccupations are related, to be sure, and run parallel through the later chapters of *The Portrait of a Lady*.

Isabel's recognition of Osmond's baleful influence on her life has moved her to the brink of "direct opposition to his wishes," as she expresses it in chapter 45, but to the brink only, for "constantly present to her mind were all the traditionary decencies and sanctities of marriage" (386). As she looks at the conflict between her desire to visit the dying Ralph and her sense of Osmond's disapproval of such action, she concludes: "It was not that she loved Ralph the less, but that almost anything seemed preferable to repudiating the most serious act—the single sacred act—of her life" (386). Once she has gone beyond that brink and announced to Osmond her firm intention of going to England to see Ralph, Osmond announces his unequivocal opposition. At this Isabel thinks, "they were married, for all that, and marriage meant that a woman should cleave to the man with whom, uttering tremendous vows, she had stood at the altar" (449). The sanctities of marriage, the sacred act, the tremendous vows—all these, her conception of the institution, the sacrament, weigh heavily with Isabel.

There is, nevertheless, another side to her view of the situation. As early as chapter 42, the initial moment of recognition—of *anagnorisis,* as the tragic dramatist used to call it—when she reviews her marriage to Gilbert, Isabel is moved to consider that "there was more in the bond than she had meant to put her name to . . ." (360). Further, in the long passage in chapter 45 in which she considers the possibility of direct confrontation with her husband and the shadow that move would cast on the "sacred act," she reiterates the suggestion that her vows covered more than she perhaps intended and might therefore have to be retracted. The whole context—and the light cast on Osmond's share in those vows—merits attention. Isabel accepts the social convention, that "he was her appointed and inscribed master," and recognizes the "decencies and sanctities of marriage": "The idea of violating them filled her with shame as well as with dread, for in giving herself away she had lost sight of this contingency in the perfect belief that her husband's intentions were as generous as her own. She seemed to see, none the less, the rapid approach of the day when she would have to take back something she had solemnly bestown" (386). She even specifies the conditions under which that day might arrive, focusing clearly as she does so on her wish to see Ralph. "Ralph never said a word against him, but Osmond's sore, mute protest was none the less founded. If he should positively interpose, if he should put forth his authority, she would have to decide, and that wouldn't be easy" (386).

Osmond does of course "interpose," and his rhetoric derives a good deal of its effectiveness from echoing Isabel's own concern. "I take our marriage seriously," he declares, and adds, "I think we should accept the consequences of our acts, and what I value most in life is the honour of a thing!" (446). In the account of Isabel's response to this eloquent and hypocritical outburst, James carefully and subtly yet quite clearly distinguishes certain important features: he indicates that Isabel is perfectly aware of the seriousness of his declaration but that she can see it for what it truly is—a consistent continuation of the attitude she has recognized in chapter 42. She also acknowledges the temptation presented by her own generosity and indeed respect for the sanctity of her avowed commitment in the wedding ceremony. We must be careful not to be taken in by Osmond's *performance*—a danger Isabel perceives lucidly. She dwells on the last words of his oration, "the honour of a thing": "though she felt that any expression of respect on his part could only be a refinement of egotism, they [his "last words"] represented something transcendent and absolute, like the sign of the cross or the flag of one's country. He spoke in the name of something sacred and precious—the observation of a magnificent form" (446). Form.

Isabel's thoughts invite us to distinguish between *form* and *essence*—between, for example, the wedding *ceremony* and the commitment it represents, or the marriage *vows* and the moral intention they are supposed to embody. The careful expression of her thoughts indicates an equation of Osmond's words with "the sign of the cross or the flag of one's country" and Osmond's implicit idea that these are "transcendent and absolute." Osmond has typically attended to *the sign* rather than to what it truly signifies: as he early confessed to Isabel, he is not conventional but "convention itself."

Her thoughts continue, insisting again on the paradox or irony of Osmond's declaration and his actual commitment, and indicating the temptation she must resist: "her old passion for justice still abode within her; and now, in the very thick of her sense of *her husband's blasphemous sophistry*, it began to throb to a tune which *for a moment promised him the victory*. It came over her that in his wish to preserve appearances he was after all sincere, and that as far as it went was a merit" (446; my italics). Osmond's commitent to the superficial and cosmetic, to the form rather than to the essence, combines with his "blasphemous sophistry," especially concerning the sacred bond of their marriage, to convince Isabel that those vows are thereby rendered invalid. The development in the concluding chapters of the novel shows that the conditions requiring new decisions respecting her marriage and obedience to the "tremendous vows" have been fulfilled; Isabel therefore acts according to her own wishes concerning visits to Ralph whether ill in Rome or dying back at Gardencourt. For Osmond *did* "interpose" and "put forth his authority" (386), and she consequently *did* "take back something she had solemnly bestown" in going to Ralph. The throb of her sense of "justice," promising Osmond "the victory," lasted only "for a moment" and Isabel *did* leave—specifically against Osmond's will—and go to Ralph.

Isabel has thus emphatically demonstrated her freedom from Osmond's domination and distinctly reaffirmed her originally cherished independence and self-reliance. A most important difference must be noted, however: that self upon which Isabel once again decides to rely is by no means the naive, innocent, ignorant self she once flaunted so charmingly at Gardencourt. She is now a mature woman, experienced in the ways of the world, familiar with the workings of evil, knowledgeable. She has seen the ghost of Gardencourt, as Ralph foretold she might; and she now seems ready to follow his old advice, "Live as you like best" (192).

Yet she returns to Rome. It should be quite clear, however, that obedience to the marriage she once held sacred is no longer the motivating force. The only sense of duty and obligation that remains to motivate Isabel is the *mature* sense of duty to herself, of enlightened self-interest. A triumph for James's "new woman"—perhaps for even more than that!

There also remains, nevertheless, the nagging memory of two apparently contradictory passages—contradictory of each other and, together, of the evident development of Isabel's liberation—to be attended to. Her announcement to Osmond that she intends to go to England to see Ralph produces this exchange:

> "I suppose that if I go you'll not expect me to come back," said Isabel.
> He turned quickly around . . . and then, "Are you out of your mind?" he enquired.
> "How can it be anything but a rupture?" she went on; "especially if all you say is true?" She was unable to see how it could be anything but a rupture: she sincerely wished to know what else it might be. (447)

Her conversation with Ralph, just before his death, would seem to indicate that she has changed her mind, or perhaps discovered something of "what else it might be":

> "Oh yes, I've been punished," Isabel sobbed.
> He listened to her a little, and then continued: "Was he very bad about your coming?"
> "He made it very hard for me. But I don't care."
> "It is all over then between you."
> "Oh no, I don't think anything's over." (478)

But when Ralph then asks whether she will go back to Osmond, Isabel answers, "I don't know."

Quickly enough there follow the appearance of the ghost, the last temptation as provided by Goodwood's kiss, and Henrietta's announcement that "this morning she started for Rome" (490). And one is tempted, maybe, to say that James *has* left things up in the air, has *not* seen his heroine to the end of her situation—just as he predicted in his notebooks that readers would say. What sort of "rupture" is it that is no rupture; what has Isabel's leaving Osmond meant if she now does not "think anything's over"; and is the marriage of the Osmonds still in effect and as lethally meaningful as ever? Are the vows she retracted now back in force? There is certainly something paradoxical here.

Perhaps the paradox associated with the first of the two preoccupations I mentioned as running roughly parallel to each other is aided by the second of those preoccupations, the question of whether Isabel married of her own "free will" or whether she was manipulated into that marriage by Madame Merle. As early as chapter 33 the question is raised when Mrs. Touchett supposes Isabel is going to marry "Madame Merle's friend—Mr. Osmond"; she amplifies that for Isabel's benefit:

> "If he's not her friend he ought to be—after what she has done for him!" cried Mrs. Touchett. "I shouldn't have expected it of her; I'm disappointed."
> "If you mean that Madame Merle has had anything to do with my engagement you're greatly mistaken," Isabel declared with a sort of ardent coldness. (282)

Some time later Isabel recalls this exchange, just before coming upon Serena and Gilbert together in silent communion, appropriately enough, the scene that provokes her long vigil in chapter 42. Her attitude has altered little in the interval. "Isabel had had three years to think over Mrs. Touchett's theory that Madame Merle had made Gilbert Osmond's marriage. . . . Madame Merle might have made Gilbert Osmond's marriage, but she had certainly not made Isabel Archer's" (339). The development of Isabel's attitude continues, with Isabel insistent on having made her choice freely, or at least without external pressure: "It was impossible to pretend that she had not acted with her eyes open; if ever a girl had been a free agent she had been. A girl in love was doubtless not a free agent; but the sole source of her mistake had been within herself. There had been no plot, no snare; she had looked and considered and chosen" (340).

That brave claim is altered, however, by the jarring interview she has with Serena Merle on the matter of securing Warburton for Pansy. The shocking recognition that Serena's interest coincides with Gilbert's provokes her to ask "What have you to do with me?" and the sharp, curt reply "Everything!" prompts Isabel to conclude "that Mrs. Touchett was right. Madame Merle had married her" (430). The final interview between these women, at the convent in which Pansy has been incarcerated, gives Isabel her modest revenge but really doesn't do much to answer unambiguously the question at issue. When Serena tells Isabel that Ralph was responsible for the inheritance that made her so eminently marriageable, Isabel's reply—her only revenge—is, "I believed it was you I had to thank!" (464).

We seem to be left with the question unanswered: either the manipulating Madame Merle made Isabel's marriage or Isabel made a free choice under no influence other than being in love! We are left with one additional perplexing response to ponder. Back in chapter 40, when she is recalling Mrs. Touchett's notion that Serena was to blame for the marriage and Isabel is again denying it in her own mind, she adds a strange explanation—that while Madame Merle might have made Osmond's marriage, "she certainly had not made Isabel Archer's. That was the work of—Isabel scarcely knew what: of nature, providence, fortune, of the eternal mystery of things" (339). One might dismiss this explanation as a bit of wistful whimsy were it not for the resonance of that echoing final phrase. James informs us in the preface to *The Portrait of a Lady* that he had begun the novel with "the conception of a certain young woman affronting her destiny" (8)—facing her fortune, what providence provides her—but says nothing about "the eternal mystery of things." Yet he does use that phrase a little earlier in the novel and in such a way as to focus and perhaps assist our perception. On his first visit to Mrs. Osmond, Ralph is struck with a particular quality of her appearance—that she is completely masked, decked out to create an impression, decorated so as to represent something. Ralph concludes she represents Osmond: "'Good heavens, what a function,' he then woefully exclaimed. He was lost in wonder at the mystery of things" (331).

Henry James was certainly no more a determinist—and even less a fatalist—than was his philosopher brother William. But he might have meant by that phrase about the mystery of things a sort of equivalent to "providence," "fortune," or "destiny." In any case, I want to propose this perception of Isabel's as the teasing answer James offers to the question—that her marriage was indeed the work of "the eternal mystery of things." And I would propose further that this teasing answer is a bold indication of what the novel is "all about," what its broadly relevant implications amount to.

In figurative terms, Isabel Archer's marriage to Gilbert Osmond is a *necessary* step to maturity, and a condition of Isabel's maturity is her recognizing that necessity—and recognizing further that while the *nature* of that marriage can be altered (there is the arena for the possible exercise of freedom), the marriage itself must be maintained, even if (as is to be hoped) in an altered state.[8]

6

The Lady in the Portrait

Many interesting explanations of the basic "meaning" of *The Portrait of a Lady* rely on the application of a set of terms more or less analogous to the "terms" of James's narrative. We all tend to do that sort of thing when we try to make more understandable an unfamiliar proposal or set of instructions: "You know," we say, "it's as though I said to you . . . ," and then rephrase the original in terms familiar to our audience. One of the most satisfactory of such explanations is that developed by Paul B. Armstrong in *The Phenomenology of Henry James* (1983). He begins with questions similar to those we have been dealing with: "what is the relationship between our will and our fate, our possibilities and their limits, our freedom and the demands of necessity? These are questions James is forever posing in his fiction as he probes this paradoxical aspect of experience."[9]

Now this is not in itself a new approach to James and to *The Portrait of a Lady,* as Armstrong admits: "almost every critic who has written about Isabel," he notes, "has done so in terms of freedom and necessity" (Armstrong, 101). He mentions specifically Dorothy Van Ghent and others like Arnold Kettle as foremost among such critics; then he adds this explanation: "My reading of *The Portrait* will try to lay bare the experiential underpinnings of the issue—the origins of the dialectic of freedom and in the basic structure of existence as James understands it" (Armstrong, 101). Those "origins" are the writings of existential phenomenologists such as Martin Heidegger, Maurice Merleau-Ponty, and Paul Ricoeur, and also of William James, elder brother of Henry James. The relevant ideas, and the terms typically used to express them, are that at birth we find ourselves "cast" into a world that is already decided for us; the limitations of the "ground" upon which we are "cast" are simply present at birth and our "field of possibility" is thus restricted. That is not cause for gloom, however:

> We always have the freedom to take a critical posture towards our ground and thereby to accept it as a field that allows the option of trying to change it. . . . But if, in what Ricoeur calls a "dream of innocence," we refuse to "consent to necessity," we not only delude ourselves about our possibilities but, even worse, actually sacrifice our freedom by fleeing from its conditions of possibility. (Armstrong, 100)

The road to satisfactory maturity—escaping from that dream of innocence, consenting to the restrictions of "necessity," enjoying what true freedom results in consequence—is described helpfully in related terms offered by William James. (1) The "healthy-minded," "once-born" individual—living the dream of innocence—is naively confident of possessing the power to realize limitless potential, sees the world as good and full of readily achievable objectives. That soul has to recognize the "tragic" fact of human existence, inescapable limitations, intervening evil. (2) That recognition produces a condition of near despair, the "sick soul" who almost loses faith in any sort of freedom, in the existence of any realizable possibilities at all. (3) The "twice-born" perseveres, reflecting on actual conditions and the yet realizable potential within them, and achieves that freedom which results, paradoxically, from the recognition of necessity; and that is a more profound, more mature and more exalted freedom, of course, than was dreamed of in the state of innocence. On that paradoxical achievement Armstrong comments, "Ricoeur summarizes this reciprocity between freedom and necessity in what he calls 'the paradox of the servile will.' Servitude and the will go hand in hand" (Armstrong, 100–101).

Even such a simplified sketch as this readily indicates the applicability of this system of belief to the career of Isabel Archer, and Armstrong's application of it attempts (and with commendable success, it seems to me) to reveal "how Isabel's story dramatizes the paradox of the servile will" (Armstrong, 103).

The Isabel who makes her entry at Gardencourt is the very embodiment of the "healthy-minded" creature William James describes. The novel carefully alerts us, from the outset, to the serious omissions from Isabel's experience. When Mrs. Touchett visited her in Albany, the young Isabel "had had the best of everything" and had already discovered that "it was an advantage never to have known anything particularly unpleasant. It appeared to Isabel that the unpleasant had been even too absent from her knowledge" (39). Again, from the opening line of chapter 4, James exposes Isabel's inexperience, naïveté, and ill-founded satisfaction with herself and focuses especially on the signal lack of knowledge of the unpleasant, of *evil*: "On the whole, reflectively, she was in no uncertainty about the things that were wrong. She had no love of their look, but when she fixed them hard she recognised them. It was wrong to be mean, to be jealous, to be false, to be cruel; *she had seen very little of the evil of the world,* but she had seen women who had tried to hurt each other" (54; my italics). Her knowledge of evil, like her idea of liberty, is "theoretic" (145).

Her reputation for independence has preceded her to Gardencourt, and once arrived, she demonstrates her naive confidence in herself and her right to virtually limitless freedom and unrestricted choice at every turn. She rejects the marriage proposals of Lord Warburton and Caspar Goodwood as threats to her freedom. Her debate with Madame Merle, as we have seen, further exposes Isabel's rejection of any external limitations; she claims, "nothing else expresses me. Nothing that belongs to me is any measure of me; everything's on the contrary a limit, a barrier, and a perfectly arbitrary one" (175).

It might seem that old Mr. Touchett's bequest of £70,000 has truly enabled Isabel to exercise something like the absolute freedom she claims. In chapter 31 she has the distinct·sense that "The world lay before her—she could do whatever she chose" (273); consequently she and Madame Merle set off on an extended tour: "Isabel travelled rapidly and recklessly; she was like a thirsty person draining cup after cup" (274). But the key word "recklessly" and the interjected "like" combine to tell a different story. The imagery of draining the cup is reminiscent of that used when Ralph urges her to "see life" at the close of chapter 15: there, we recall, he suggests that she wants "to drain the cup of experience"; she denies this firmly: "It's a poisoned drink! I only want to see for myself"; Ralph's quiet comment makes the point: "You want to see but not to feel" (134). Innocent freedom indeed! Isabel's actually seeing for herself is done rapidly and *recklessly*—that is, heedlessly, inattentively, unhelpfully; and she is *not*, we must notice, a thirsty person draining the cup, but "*like* a thirsty person," an imitation of the real thing. She evidently learns little from the tour.

Continuing in her dream of innocence, Isabel accepts Gilbert Osmond's proposal of marriage in part because it seems to promise her an escape from life's threatening limitations. That crucial step gives Isabel ample opportunity to discover the evil of the world in all its dreadful entirety and with all its most restrictive limitations. The vigil in chapter 42 begins Isabel's long-drawn-out recognition that "to seek possibility without limits means to find limits without possibility" (Armstrong, 120). Thus she enters the phase of the "sick soul," faced with the intimidating reality of evil in the world, and threatened by despair. In this position she seems caught between two alternatives: she can remain submissive to the forces she has surrendered to in marrying Osmond or she can become defiant and rebellious against them. To remain submissive is to deny that she has any freedom at all; to rebel is to deny the responsibility of recognizing that limits do exist. She must seek a compromise between these polar alternatives that will allow her both to recognize her responsibility to exercise what freedom is available and to admit what limitations are inevitable. To achieve that position, possible to the "twice-born," is to acknowledge and work within the "paradox of the servile will."

Isabel's first clear moment of success, indicating her development into the condition of the "twice-born," is her meeting with Madame Merle at the convent (chapter 52). Isabel knows the truth about Serena and sees that Serena realizes this (458); she has refused to yield to Osmond's old friend and likewise to oppose her defiantly, to seek revenge; as noted, she merely confronts Serena. By the same token, however, Isabel's leaving Rome must be seen as an act of defiance against Osmond and his wishes and a demonstration that she has not yet firmly accepted the paradox of the servile will.

What this reading of *The Portrait of a Lady* can now offer us is an explanation of Isabel's decision to return to Rome—and all that this involves—and an indication of the significance of her choice. In a word, this decision shows that Isabel has understood, once again and finally, that her only possible freedom involves recognition of the demands of necessity. She resumes the position of success she enjoyed in merely confronting Madame Merle, neither submitting nor defying. This reading also deals with the bothersome open-endedness of the novel: Isabel's decision marks the end of her progress toward that position of success, but it also marks the beginning of a new existence consequent upon that decision. Armstrong explains: "As a figure of the servile will, Isabel shows that discovering a right relation between freedom and necessity does not end our conflicts; it only grants recognition to the terms within which we must struggle to decide our existence." And again, "Isabel must accept involvements with others who are hostile or solicitous as part of the situation into which she is thrown" (Armstrong, 134, 135).

The reading made possible by the terms of the phenomenological approach clarifies much of *The Portrait of a Lady* and takes us a good way toward a satisfactory understanding of the novel. But even this reading falters, finally, when brought up against specific features of the conclusion, namely "the sexual and social inadequacies of the novel's ending" (Armstrong, 133). The complaint mentions Isabel's "arbitrary and incompletely chosen . . . consent to the obligations of marriage" (Armstrong, 128): "because of James's attitude toward the politics of social reality, Isabel is never given the chance to regard her marriage as a cultural contingency that she might choose to criticize and struggle against. . . . Isabel never really enjoys the possibility of attacking critically the institutional arrangement that justifies Osmond's power over her" (Armstrong, 132). Coupled with this view is the perception of Isabel "as a frigid young girl who . . . finds the only kiss in the book (Goodwood's) hysterically disturbing because of her intensely ambivalent enjoyment and *fear of passion*" (Armstrong, 132; my italics). Freud is understandably invoked in an effort to clarify this problem:

> for Freud, consciousness must accept the body's libidinal endowment as an inescapable part of its situation and attempt to tame its force to the control of meaning. To flee from one's sexual impulses (as Isabel does) is to increase one's bondage to them. . . . Like the limits of her attitude toward marriage, though, the flaws in Isabel's sexual understanding are undoubtedly to some extent James's too. (Armstrong, 133)

So there we are.

Another example of the use of analogous terminology is offered by Virginia C. Fowler in *James's American Girl* (1984). There, her application of Freudian revisionist Jacques Lacan's theories of child development brings her reading of *The Portrait of a Lady* into close parallel with Armstrong's phenomenological reading. Fowler indicates that the Jamesian heroine rejects identity as a subjective "I"; that is, she would deny mature recognition of the distinction between Self and Other. That denial, in favor of the illusory "unified ego," matches the attitude of the "healthy-minded," "once-born" individual (to recall the terms of William James as Armstrong uses them) and also Isabel's initial belief in the possibility of limitless freedom: denial of the separate, objective existence of the Other is the equivalent of a denial of necessity, of a refusal to recognize the defining and limiting features of human existence.

Knowledge of the objective Other is painful and frightening; it means the loss of the condition of innocence and ignorance—the state of childhood, of the "unified ego," the "healthy-minded" soul. Achieving and accepting that knowledge is, however, a necessary step toward maturity and full participation in the human condition. And Fowler's application of Lacanian theory involves the use of some other interesting and otherwise familiar terms: "If, in fact, the fear of the suffering accompanying knowledge or 'awareness' makes Americans in general and the American girl in particular unnaturally prolong their blissful state of unawareness, then the trauma the American girl experiences when she is invited *to eat of 'the tree of knowledge'* which she finds in Europe perhaps becomes more explicable" (I italicize the term in question, for we will want to recall it later).[10] Not to reject necessary knowledge, not to fear the suffering that comes with the embracing of experience (and that is a moment like the period of near despair felt by William James's "sick soul" and the equivalent of Isabel's midnight vigil in chapter 42) leads to the enrichment of consciousness that characterizes human maturity—the condition of the "twice-born" and of what William Blake called "higher innocence."

Not only does this schematization of Isabel's career correspond rather closely to that of Armstrong; it seems quite faithful to the features of the novel as we all would read it. In spite of all, however, Fowler finds the ending of *The Portrait* as unsatisfactory as does Armstrong; the interesting difference is that she faults the realistic mode of the novel for that failing:

> marriage [in *The Portrait*] seems to operate on two different levels: on the level of the universal, James treats marriage almost as a metaphor for a commitment to life itself . . . ; on the level of the particular, however, he boldly delineates the specific horrors that arise from the various marriages in the novel. . . . Isabel Archer cannot resolve the opposition because it inheres in James's own inconsistent attitudes and beliefs. James resolved it for himself, surely, by virtue of his being a man and of his commitment to art; as Quentin Anderson has observed, . . . it was "impossible to make Isabel Archer over into a man and launch her on the career of an artist." . . . For her, as for most women of the nineteenth century, such an escape from marriage was impossible. (Fowler, 68–69)

This seems an odd attitude, especially in view of that interesting reference to "the level of the universal"; furthermore, one might respond that Henry James evidently understood the term "artist" in quite the way his father did: "He alone is the Artist, whatever be his manifest vocation, whose action obeys his own internal taste or attraction, uncontrolled by necessity or duty."[11] Fowler also seems to confound her own impressive argument by insisting that Isabel's "commitment is to life, and her life exists where she has created it, in her marriage to Gilbert Osmond," and by offering as explanation that "At best the American girl treated in realistic fiction can have but a muted triumph because the powers of her femininity and her consciousness are inevitably limited by the world the fiction forces her to inhabit" (Fowler, 81, 82).

One is tempted to say that the problem of the opposition of the universal to the particular (in terms of James's marriages in his fiction) or of the opposition of the metaphoric and the realistic is not finally Isabel's or James's problem but much rather the problem of the critic or the general reader. But Professor Fowler raises such an interesting and pertinent question here that it must be further addressed before I proceed to offer another analogous application to a reading of *The Portrait of a Lady*. We might begin by recalling the evident distinction James makes in his essay "The Art of Fiction" between "the look of things" and "the look that conveys their meaning," which we glanced at briefly in chapter 3.

That distinction is immanent in a similar comment James made in his preface to *The Tragic Muse*. A familiar passage addresses the importance of artistry, that is, of formal structure, of strong "composition," for a novel; without that, the preface claims, one is left with just life—the raw material of art:

> A picture without composition slights its most precious chance for beauty, and is moreover not composed at all unless the painter knows *how* that principle of health and safety, working as an absolutely premeditated art, has prevailed. There may in its absence be life, incontestably, as "The Newcomes" has life, as "Les Trois

Mousquetaires," as Tolstoi's "Peace and War" [*sic*], have it; but what do such large loose baggy monsters, with their queer elements of the accidental and the arbitrary artistically *mean*? . . . There is life and life, and as waste is only life sacrificed and thereby prevented from "counting," I delight in a deep-breathing economy and an organic form.[12]

James's short story of 1892 "The Real Thing" canvases the same distinction. The painter in that story fails in his illustrations when he is dictated to by his models (Major and Mrs. Monarch), who are actually, realistically, what he wants to paint—the "real thing." The models are *only* themselves, real lady and gentleman (though now down on their luck); the painter's Cockney girl and Italian boy are suggestive and expressive, they represent—not reproduce—what he needs. The paintings he makes from them, Miss Churm and Oronte, are in turn meaningfully expressive and suggestive, are not prevented from "counting." *The Portrait of a Lady*, I submit, is of that sort of nonrealistic art, ultimately, even though its almost too satisfactory surface makes it look like a traditional "realistic" novel.

A number of modern critics not of the neohistorical stamp have more readily grasped and appreciated the distinction in question. We have already (in chapter 3) noted briefly Annette T. Rubenstein's claim that James was *not* a "traditional realistic novelist." She amplifies that claim by arguing that James *was,* "at his best,"

like Cooper, Hawthorne and Melville, and unlike Defoe, Fielding, Austen, Dickens and Eliot, an abstract or metaphysical novelist. It is easy for us to see that so naive a novelist as Cooper still lives not because of, but rather in spite of, his clumsy dialogue, romantic Indians and creaky plots. Though he does undeniably have a real flair for presenting scenes of crowded violent action, there would be little loss if we were to ignore virtually everything but the heroic myth of Deerslayer. This fixed in a moment of pure poetry the new man, without forebears or descendants, face to face with the virgin forests of a new world—forests and a world that were doomed to vanish almost as rapidly as he himself did. (Rubinstein, 318)

The Lady in the Portrait

The phrase "a moment of pure poetry" is surely eloquent, and it brings to mind one of the most satisfactory comments of all on this whole matter and explains why the problem in understanding James is *ours* in our demand for "the real" and our blindness to metaphor or to poetry in novel form.

In commenting on Cervantes' *Don Quixote* and specifically on the conflict between the Don and his companion Sancho Panza—the conflicting claims of literature and life—Leo Spitzer observes that

> that hybrid genre of the novel is born of poetry and of something else, of an extrapoetic factor, of a tendency to encroach upon life, along with an inborn striving toward pure art, a nostalgic yearning back to epic beauty. The older form of narration is everywhere epic poetry, epic poetry that maintains itself in the sphere of pure art, of a stylization of life, without any direct imitation or caricature of life. . . .
>
> But the novel can offer a vicarious life to sap our actual life, and produce an illusion in which the things narrated appear as present, and the lines between romance and reality are blurred. The prosaic form contributes to this illusion, making romance appear as authentic, unaltered reality.[13]

It should be obvious that Spitzer is not here distinguishing between "romance" and the "realistic novel." One can see, thus, that the problem lies in the eye of the beholder who wants to see fiction as biography or history and not with the novel that James has so artfully created.

Perhaps another kind of reading, close to but yet distinct from the two excellent readings we have just been looking at, can answer the objections raised by Armstrong and Fowler. My discussion of the ending of *The Portrait* (in chapter 5) may already have answered these objections to some extent, but applying the other set of analogous terms, suggested by the novel itself (and by the overlooked essay I mentioned earlier, "*The Portrait of a Lady*: 'The Eternal Mystery of Things,'" 1959)—the "eternal mystery" approach—may provide a more satisfactory solution to the "problems" of the ending and indeed to the meaning of the whole novel. The phenomenological approach uses some of those terms, and certainly Henry James's brother William used them—understandably.

Professor Armstrong refers approvingly to earlier Jamesian critics Dorothy Van Ghent and Arnold Kettle. They also are familiar with the terms in question. Van Ghent observes that the essence of *The Portrait of a Lady* "is contained in the words, 'He that loses his life shall find it'"; Kettle comments that the novel might be called "a nineteenth-century *Paradise Lost.*"[14] The terms in question (like William James's "once-born," "sick soul," and "twice-born") come from the Judeo-Christian tradition, and especially from the Protestant Christian tradition that includes not just Milton's *Paradise Lost* and *Paradise Regained* but William Blake's *Songs of Innocence* and *Songs of Experience,* Nathaniel Hawthorne's *The Marble Faun,* and even Henry James, Sr.'s *The Secret of Swedenborg* and *Society the Redeamed Form of Man.* We have already noted that Goodwood's statement to Isabel, "The world's all before us" (489), is a distinct echo of the last sentence of *Paradise Lost* (as well as of Isabel's much earlier claim, 273). We should now be able to recognize that *The Portrait* is chock-full of similar terms that comprise a broad and firm network; they are not obtrusive, are in fact so artfully embedded in the narrative surface, so carefully "concealed" in the metaphoric utterance—the look of things—that we tend not to notice them much. But we have already looked at a number of them: I have quoted several, though without always (or even often) so identifying them.

Isabel Archer enters the scene at Gardencourt. The name now seems appropriate as the Edenic setting of Isabel's initial innocence. A subtle but now clearly recognizable emphasis pervades the opening description of Gardencourt (I add italics here to point that up):

[The implements of afternoon tea] had been disposed upon the lawn of an old English country-house, in ... the *perfect* middle of a splendid summer afternoon. ... the shadows were long upon the smooth, dense turf. They lengthened slowly, however, and the scene expressed that *sense of leisure still to come* which is perhaps the chief source of one's enjoyment at such an hour. From five o'clock to eight is on certain occasions *a little eternity*; but on such occasions as this the interval could only be *an eternity of pleasure*. . . . The shadows on the *perfect* lawn. . . . (17)

And so on; the whole opening paragraph is redolent of Edenic bliss.

As the innocent Isabel leaves Gardencourt to embark on her career the novel sets up its principal geographic opposition. Isabel's experience takes her to Gilbert Osmond and Rome, which she comes to think of "chiefly as the place where people had suffered" (430). We may take Rome as standing for the world—the fallen world outside of Eden, or of Gardencourt. Here the married Isabel lives, and specifically "in the very heart of Rome"; and here she suffers the shock of recognition that opens her eyes to the situation she has put herself in as Mrs. Osmond. Her career follows the three stages marked by William James as we have seen them; Henry James, however, encourages us to see them in Blakean (or Miltonic) terms as (1) innocence, (2) experience, and (3) maturity or "higher innocence" or "salvation." And Isabel's moving from (1) to (2) is pointedly characterized as a *fall* from innocence. Ralph has encouraged her, fondly, to spread her wings and rise above the ground (192); after her engagement he tries one last time to dissuade her from marrying Osmond: "'You were not to come down so easily. . . . It hurts me,' said Ralph audaciously, 'hurts me *as if I had fallen myself*'" (291; my italics). She must face the truth about the evil to which she has wedded herself—not flee from the fact like Blake's Thel; and as she begins to do so, in chapter 42, the familiar terminology is resumed. Two features predominate: her sense of having "fallen," having "come down," and her sense of the darkness in which she now dwells. We have already considered James's depiction of Osmond as a figure something like the Prince of Darkness and the associated image of the satanic "serpent in a bank of flowers." Furthermore, we have also noted the imagery by which Ralph is contrasted to Osmond—his visit is "a lamp in the darkness" (363), he is "an apostle of freedom" whereas Osmond "wished her to have no freedom of mind" (386); "Ralph was generous and . . . made her feel the good of the world" (363–64), whereas Osmond has reaffirmed her sense of the world as "base, ignoble" (360). These are the two characters who most urgently oppose each other in a struggle to influence Isabel's mind or consciousness or soul.

That opposition pits the forces of restriction—what the phenomenological reading identifies as "necessity"—as embodied in Osmond, "convention itself," and in Madame Merle, "the great round world itself," against the force of the "apostle of freedom." James develops the forces of restriction by means of imagery taken, obviously, from the Roman Catholic church: Osmond's reiterated envy of the Pope of Rome, his approaching Isabel in St. Peter's Cathedral "with all the forms . . . multiplied . . . to suit the place," his use of the convent to educate Pansy, and so forth. We have looked at that imagery and recognized that James's use of it has virtually nothing to do with anti-Roman Catholic sentiments, that it includes Anglican features (Lord Warburton's "canoness" sister, for example) and indeed any heavily ritualized, "high church" institutions; and furthermore that Osmond's association with those features emphasizes his error, his mistaken view of them: he envies the Pope for expressly the wrong reasons and abuses the convent by making it a prison to chasten his daughter. The purpose, we have already seen, is to underline Osmond's commitment to form rather than to essence, to the mere look as opposed to the actual meaning; but that commitment is further significant, for the essence in question here, behind or within the forms of Christian religious ritual, is the essence of Christianity. Its message is the message of love. Osmond's supreme hypocrisy emerges strongly in the contrast between his attitude to the particular form that has wedded him to Isabel, and her prolonged and vexed concern over the meaning of her "tremendous vows," "the single sacred act" of her life. We should recall Osmond's bluff claim as he refuses to condone Isabel's leaving to see the dying Ralph—"I take our marriage seriously" (446)!

With Isabel's full recognition of evil in the world, the crucial moment of her experience, she wants to turn away from that evil and escape that world. Her thoughts turn to Gardencourt, and James further characterizes that location by extending the network of terms:

just before Ralph's departure from Rome, it strikes Isabel that there was "something *sacred* in Gardencourt" (414; my italics), and on her way back to England she thinks, "Gardencourt had been her starting-point, . . . it would be a *sanctuary* now" (465; my italics). Lest it seem that we have come full circle and lest we mistake the function of Gardencourt in the novel's network of expression, James has qualified both these passages (my italics): "Gardencourt; no chapter of the past was more *perfectly irrecoverable*," and "her starting-point, and to those muffled chambers it was at least a *temporary solution* to return." For Gardencourt is the scene of innocence, and that is not resumed— and not meant to be: what *is* possible is something beyond that.

She has gone there to escape Osmond and all the evil of her life with him, his commitment to the world (and perhaps with that, tra- ditionally, to the flesh and the devil). We must not overlook the sig- nificant fact that it is Ralph who has drawn her away from Rome and back to the temporary sanctuary; and with that we might rehearse briefly Ralph's role in Isabel's career to see what features of that role now will assert themselves with new meaningfulness. He early en- couraged her to rely on herself and especially to plunge into experi- ence—to "see life" and to "drain the cup of experience." He has procured for her the means of freedom—the inheritance of £70,000. That gift, its purpose, and Isabel's attitude to it combine to discover another meaningful pattern: the gift of freedom comes originally from the father although it comes to Isabel via the offices of the son. Further it is the death of that son—strictly speaking, the imminent death— that draws Isabel away from submission to the novel's Prince of Dark- ness; once at Gardencourt she must wait a period of three days (twice specified on p. 476) before full communication with Ralph is possible. This last detail is recognizably some kind of echo of the death and resurrection of Jesus, "crucified, dead, and buried. . . . The third day he rose again from the dead: He ascended into heaven," in the words of the Apostles' Creed. Then there is the fulfillment of the prophecy about the ghost of Gardencourt. That ghost will complete the signifi- cant trio—or *trinity*, if we are to be consistent with the novel's network of terms. And we have already considered the interesting confusion, in the scene of visitation, between Ralph and the ghost. I want to adapt an observation made by Martha Banta some time ago about Ralph and the ghost. She says that Isabel has earned that vision, that visitation, by "living into the experience whose meaning Ralph Touchett understands from the first—both because he has already seen the ghost and because he is, in a sense, a good ghost himself."[15] A few pages later Professor Banta wonderfully observes that Isabel "has at last been shown the way out into life by Ralph's consciousness, *even if he had to die for her to experience it fully*" (Banta, 178; my italics), as though to suggest that his death was somehow sacrificial. To insist that we have here a Jamesian equivalent of the Christian Holy Trinity—father, son, and holy ghost—would certainly be to go too far, to try to push the novel over the edge and into allegory; but to fail to see just how close James has dared to go in that direction is surely to miss the evident intention of the novel's metaphoric narrative.

In addition to all this, there is James's puzzling use of capitalized pronouns in connection with Ralph. First, in this jocular exchange between him and Henrietta regarding his attitude to Isabel:

"Well, you're not in love with her, I hope."
"How can that be, when I'm in love with *Another*?"
"You're in love with yourself, that's the *Other!*" Miss Stackpole declared. (108; my italics)

The original version has "another" and "other." Much later, as Warburton and Ralph discuss Isabel's attraction to Osmond, Ralph says grimly, "She wants nothing that we can give her." Then, "'Ah well, if she won't have You—!' said his lordship handsomely as they went" (253). Warburton's riposte was also added, with the "You," in the revision. I can point to this tantalizing use of capitalization, as if in the tradition of respect in reference to the deity—"Our Father, . . . Thy name," etc.—and indicate that it was quite obviously intentional in these instances, but I have no explanation to offer.

Of course the final gift that Isabel realizes is the gift of love—a selfless, undemanding, liberating, spiritual love. Ralph's last words to her are, "if you've been hated you've also been loved. Ah but, Isabel—*adored!*" (479). He had said to her earlier, to quiet her anguish at his dying: "You won't lose me—you'll keep me. Keep me in your heart; I shall be nearer to you than I have ever been" (477). And we should now recall, to savor the rich promise of the lightly spoken comment that we passed over as lightly earlier on, Isabel's saying to Ralph, "You were reserved for my future" (130). With all this, another exchange between her and Ralph returns with new meaning. In the midst of their discussion of whether Warburton cares for Pansy,

> "Ah, Ralph, you give me no help!" she cried abruptly and passionately.
> It was the first time she had alluded to the need for help . . . He gave a long murmur of relief . . . the gulf between them had been bridged. (388)

That abrupt, passionate cry recalls the Christian admonition, "Ask and it shall be given unto you; seek and ye shall find."

At Ralph's death Isabel is freed again to return to the world, to Rome. It should be clear that the figurative death she experienced en route to Gardencourt has been followed by a rebirth into stage (3)—maturity, "higher innocence," salvation. Her fall into experience has been the Fortunate (or Fruitful) Fall—the *felix culpa*—that one sees through that long Protestant Christian tradition from Milton on to James's own day.[16] Isabel's Paradise of innocence has been well lost. One might almost imagine that James had in mind the exchange in book 12 of *Paradise Lost* between Adam and the Archangel Michael after the unfolding of the future to Adam before his expulsion. Adam says

> O goodness infinite, goodness immense!
> That all this good of evil shall produce,
> And evil turn to good, . . . (1360–62)

Michael's explanation follows:

> . . . only add
> Deeds to thy knowledge answerable, add Faith
> . . . add Love,
> . . . the soul
> Of all the rest, then wilt thou not be loath
> To leave this Paradise, but shalt possess
> A Paradise within thee, happier farr. (1472–78)

So Milton has in a sense fulfilled the promise of the opening lines of his epic to rehearse the story of the fruit of the Forbidden Tree and the bringing of death and all our woe,

> With loss of *Eden,* till one greater Man
> Restore us, and regain the blissful Seat, . . . (4–5)

In *The Portrait of a Lady* Ralph Touchett plays the role of that "greater Man." His gift to Isabel has helped her to discover the *way* in which she may change (not by leaving Osmond—"one can't change that way") and the *other* reason for returning to Rome (not the reason of having promised Pansy—"perhaps I shall find another"). And if it be asked what Isabel can possibly *do* when she goes back to Rome, back into the world and to Osmond, the answer is surely implied in those lines of chapter 42 in which Isabel considers Osmond's pretended and actual attitudes to the world: "this base, ignoble world, it appeared, was after all what one was to live for; one was to keep it forever in one's eye, in order not *to enlighten or convert or redeem it,* but to extract from it some recognition of one's own superiority" (360). There we have, in that string of infinitives I have italicised, a brief and general outline of the work of the twice-born or the reborn, the sojourner who has come out on the other side of submissiveness to experience and into maturity, into "salvation." The pattern of the Christian view of the Fortunate Fall, of the development from innocence onward into adult maturity seems, then, to inform *The Portrait of a Lady.* James's international theme regularly follows that development via the medium of the apparent opposition between Americans and Europe—between the innocent and the world of experience.

James's apparently inconsequential dribbling away at the close of his preface to *The Portrait* thus takes on a new meaning: "I had, within the few preceding years, come to live in London, and the 'international' light lay, in those days, to my sense, thick and rich upon the scene. It was the light in which so much of the picture hung. But that *is* another matter. There is really too much to say" (15). Yes. Let the novel speak for itself; it does so, eloquently.

What of the ending and those two worrisome features that plagued the Lacanian and phenomenological readings? What urges Isabel to return, after all is said and done? Surely she is led by the spirit of Ralph and his adoration—as Merton Densher will be at the end of *The Wings of the Dove* by the memory of Milly Theale, and as James himself manifestly was by the memory of *his* cousin Minny Temple—led not so much away from the world as from commitment or submission to the world, from commitment to the world, the flesh, and the devil. Caspar's appeal to Isabel at the last is surely unambiguous and Isabel's response is clear: she is moved, sexually roused. In fleeing from Caspar she is not fleeing from her "sexual impulse," not denying the "body's libidinal endowment," but fleeing from the temptation to *submit* to that impulse to the extent that she would *give herself up* to it (suffer, indeed, a "re-death" after her newly achieved re-birth) when she now has so much to do—or to be.

It ought also to be clear that Isabel's return to Osmond is anything but a submitting to "the obligations of marriage." To say that "Isabel's plight is 'a paradigm' of 'Victorian woman's terrible dilemma in marriage'" (Armstrong, 132) may be true enough. That view restricts us, however, to the narrative surface of the novel, renders opaque the novel's eloquent metaphor, confines us to the mere "look of things" rather than liberating us to "the look that conveys their meaning." Besides, it also overlooks the fact that Isabel does not yield to that "plight," as we have already seen when we pondered earlier her struggle with her "tremendous vows." When Ralph asks her, after she announces she ought to return to England with him, whether fear of her husband deters her she answers boldly (it will be recalled) that she is afraid only of herself: "If I were afraid of my husband that would be simply my duty. *That's what women are expected to be*" (419; my italics). Then her direct and specific response to Osmond's extravagant and hypocritical declaration—which speaks immediately to her own concerns about those vows of hers—richly denies her succumbing to "the intellectual arrangement that justifies Osmond's power over her" (Armstrong, 132). Osmond: "I think we should accept the consequences of our actions, and what I value most in life is the honour of a thing!" Isabel's response: "her old passion for justice still abode within her; and now, in the very thick of *her sense of her husband's blasphemous sophistry*, it began to throb to a tune which *for a moment* promised to give him the victory" (446; my italics). And for a moment only, the implication surely is.

One might further argue, keeping these two associated readings vividly in mind, that while Isabel is by no means motivated by obedience to the obligations of the marriage vows in her decision to return to Rome, nevertheless the *fact* of marriage as one of the "givens" of her "ground" may yet play a motivational role. Lest this sound like double-talk, let me urge again my proposal that "the eternal mystery of things" is here at issue. In the metaphoric structure of *The Portrait of a Lady* Isabel's marriage to Osmond is necessary and even inevitable: it represents a quality of the human condition in a fallen world. A good hard look at a part of Isabel's reaction to Ralph's lament that in engaging to marry Osmond she has "fallen"—and it hurts him as if he had fallen himself—may be helpful: "You talk about one's soaring and sailing, but *if one marries at all one touches the earth.* One has *human feelings and needs,* one has a heart in one's bosom, and one must marry a particular individual" (293; my italics).

In the process of moving from initial innocence to adult maturity, each of us has to marry the "Osmond" in our world and come to terms with him—not flee from him. "Poor human-hearted Isabel" has already (and, as I say, necessarily) become *his* woman (as Serena had) as she comes to him "with charged hands" to take possession—in that act of ostensible charity—of this "subtlest manly organism" as "her property" (358); and with the best intentions she yet meant to manipulate him. Her act is reflexive, and diabolically so: Osmond's baleful attraction provoked the act, and in her attempt to gain possession of him she gives up *her* freedom. Of course all freedom is contingent. In embracing Osmond she has in effect embraced the human condition. So the "eternal mystery" may be defined: it is the condition of life in the fallen world, it made Isabel's marriage, it made her represent Osmond until she decided, with Ralph's help, to be submissive no longer to "Satan's power," not to resort to futile flight (whither?—the world, fallen or not, remains *there*) but to return to Rome and Osmond (and Pansy as well) to confront the evil of the world—to affront her destiny, confidently and not submissively.

Although she seems finally to undercut her own argument, Virginia C. Fowler offers these acute observations, which apparently support the claims I have just made:

> The final chapters of the *Portrait* attest that Isabel's marriage and, more important, her continuation in it, do in fact, in her mind, constitute her commitment to life itself. . . . during her journey from Rome . . . "she envied Ralph his dying. . . ." . . . What Isabel finds attractive in death is the cessation of knowing and of the pain which knowledge often brings. . . . The resistance to knowledge and consequent suffering . . . is thus overcome by Isabel Archer. (Fowler, 78)

> Isabel's return to her marriage to Osmond thus reflects her acceptance of what she believes the conditions of life to be. She believes that a permanent retreat or escape from Osmond would constitute a desire to escape from the realities of life itself. (Fowler, 80–81)

A final word on the heroine. At least since Philip Rahv called Isabel Archer an Emersonian heroine in his essay of 1949, critics have made the association between that onetime Unitarian minister, advocate of serene self-reliance and friend of Henry James, Sr., and James's Isabel. As though to assist his readers to make that association also, James has left a couple of specific "clues" near the end of his impressive and crucial chapter 42 of *The Portrait*. In her enlightening review of her life with Osmond, Isabel recognizes that her husband has little respect for her mind and her opinions: "she could see he was ineffably ashamed of her. . . . It had not been in his prevision of things that she should reveal such flatness; her sentiments were worthy of a radical newspaper or a Unitarian preacher" (362). The next paragraph continues that association: "It was very simple; he despised her; she had no traditions and the moral horizon of a Unitarian minister. Poor Isabel, who had never been able to understand Unitarianism!" (363). At this moment of her review Isabel is focusing both on the fact that she has unintentionally misled Osmond about what she is and on the unsavory expectations he has had regarding her (and especially the means she might use to "persuade" Warburton to propose marriage to Pansy). Poor human-hearted Isabel, who had seen very little of the evil of the world, has now encountered that evil directly and intimately. Osmond's expectations of her shock her profoundly as she looks at them hard: "They were hideously unclean. She was not a daughter of the Puritans, but for all that she believed in such a thing as chastity and even as decency. It would appear that Osmond was far from doing anything of the sort; some of his traditions made her push back her skirts" (362).[17] In his review of *The Correspondence of Thomas Carlyle and Ralph Waldo Emerson 1834–1872*, published in 1883, about a year after book publication of *The Portrait* (and the three passages just quoted were untouched by revision for the 1908 version), James observed that "Emerson . . . was an optimist. . . . He had a high and noble conception of good, without having, it would appear, a definite conception of evil" (*Criticism*, 1:242–43).[18] Evidently James was interested in offering a corrective to the optimistic Emersonian conception as he developed Isabel's career and so expressed the urgent necessity of recognizing and coming to terms with (that is, not denying or attempting to escape) the evil of the world.

Such a reading as I have offered, following the lead of what I find to be the terms of the novel itself, seems to illuminate *The Portrait* and to enjoy the benefits of other readings that are quite similar although the result of different approaches. I think the reading so offered answers the sharpest objections and makes satisfactory sense of Isabel's final decision—given that this is not a realistic account of a particular, *actual* young woman whose name was Isabel Archer, but rather a work of art with an impressively real-looking surface. Furthermore, this reading makes clear that the pattern of Isabel Archer's career is the pattern of development from immaturity to maturity, from innocence through experience to a Blakean higher innocence, from naïveté and ignorance to sane sophistication; if the career involves difficulty and suffering, the final goal of adult self-knowledge and self-respect is nevertheless worth the struggle—if she has been obliged to "fall" because she has "eaten of the fruit of the tree of knowledge," the fall has yet been fortunate. To call such a career tragic is surely to disregard the actual possibilities of human life.

The Portrait of a Lady is a charming and profoundly instructive representation of life, giving us the look of things—the look that conveys their meaning.

Coda

Henry James was absolutely correct about how his novel would be perceived, and his evasive-looking defense of its conclusion was perfectly sound. We need only understand what he was saying in his notes. He observed that readers would complain "that I have not seen the heroine to the end of her situation—that I have left her *en l'air.*— That is both true and false. The *whole* of anything is never told. . . ." So much is "true": he has not followed his heroine back to Rome and told us what she does there; he is not, that is to say, writing in the old tradition that ends a story with marriage and happily-ever-after or with death. Nor, that is also to say, has he given us a failed *divorce*-and-happily-ever-after novel. What is "false," however, is the claim that "it is not finished"; for "you can only take what groups together. What I have done has that unity—it groups together. It is complete in itself . . ." (*Notebooks* 15). It is finished, unified, complete, according to the promise of its title. And one of the reviewers of the original version saw that; unfortunately the critic is anonymous, but the review (published in *Harper's* for February 1882) is stunning, not only because it is perceptive and sophisticated but because it speaks informatively about a feature of *The Portrait* that has scarcely been recognized in this century—or if recognized, not fully understood. The review deserves generous quotation:

> For however admirable a portrait in colors may be, it can present its subject in one only of his attitudes, it must drape him in an unvarying garb, it must envision him with accessories that become monotonous under the unchanging fixedness, and it can only

reproduce the expression that he wore at a single moment of his life. In his contention with the limitation of his art, the painter . . . has been obliged to resort to the expedient of repeated sittings, so that his work shall not reflect a single fleeting or momentary play of expression, but shall combine those regnant and characteristic expressions which reflect the man at his best, and which may be caught by studying him in different moods and fluctuations of feeling and temperament. An artist with the pen has no need to resort to this expedient, as Mr. James demonstrates in his continuous and sustained portraiture of the heroine. . . . Instead of her repeated sittings being condensed into one final touch . . . each contributes to the completeness of the picture without detracting from its unity. And the result is a vivid and life-like portrait of a woman at different stages of her life from girlhood to womanhood, . . . yet ever remaining intrinsically the same, . . . throughout preserving . . . her distinctive and winsome individuality. (NCE, 654)

It is possible to dismiss this observation—if one has not got *The Portrait of a Lady* under one's nose or freshly in mind—as trivial: "sure, that's always the case with the main character in a novel." But reviewing one aspect of James's depiction of Isabel Archer leads to a recognition that the review is anything but trivial. The cubist painter Pablo Picasso knew of the "limitations of his art," as this reviewer puts it, and so did Picasso's friend Gertrude Stein, and so did Ms. Stein's friend Thornton Wilder (witness both his plays and his novels), and so did the writer that influenced both those writers, Henry James. Perhaps (to say it again) all artists are so aware, and the greatest find means to overcome these limitations—or at least to create that illusion. The painter, committed or restricted to space, will try to get a temporal element into his work; the writer, restricted to time, will try to get a spatial element.

In addition to the general sense of the whole novel as a portrait of Isabel, there is the particular phenomenon of the repeated "framing" of Isabel in the novel: at the beginning, toward the middle (shortly after she has become Mrs. Osmond), and in her final scene Isabel is depicted as framed in a doorway and on each of the three occasions is dressed in black. That phenomenon suggests that James had in mind something new and different in the line of literary portraiture.

Isabel first appears in the novel "in the ample doorway" leading to the lawn of Gardencourt; she is depicted as "a tall girl in a black dress" (25). In chapter 37 Ned Rosier has come to the Osmonds' house in Rome to pursue his quest for permission to marry Pansy: "He . . . met Mrs. Osmond coming out of the deep doorway. She was dressed in black velvet; . . . framed in the gilded doorway, she struck our young man as the picture of a gracious lady" (309–310). It is an important scene, indicating Isabel's sympathy with the possible marriage of Pansy and Ned, though she is unable to act on that sympathy as yet; she will soon thereafter promise to give Ned what aid she can. Finally, our last glimpse of Isabel, again at Gardencourt, is the last frame in the series. We see her seated on "a rustic bench, her hands, hanging at her sides, lost themselves in the folds of her black dress" (485); Caspar Goodwood enters and makes his impressive final appeal, and after Isabel has broken away she rushed to the house "and reached the door. Here only she paused. She looked all about her; she listened a little . . ." (489–90). James left these scenes untouched in his revisions of 1906, with the single exception of adding "ample" to the earliest of the three.

This phenomenon is more than a curiosity, more than a bit of narrative cuteness; it exemplifies what I discussed in chapter 2 as the writer's attempt to escape the chronological compulsion, to achieve the sense of simultaneity or contemporaneity. The effect of the technique is cumulative, like the series of frames in a film arranged one upon another so as to be seen not in sequence but all at once. The technique seems calculated to discourage the unwarranted (as James saw it) question "What will she do next?"—which would lead to the anticipated criticism that "this is not concluded," and instead to encourage the question it has been employed to answer, "What *is* she now?" or "What has she *become?*" By the repetition of these "framing" scenes James conveys the impression of accumulated events simultaneously perceived. The three scenes are signally representative of Isabel's *state of being* at a given moment. In the first she is the newly arrived innocent; in the second she is no longer the innocent but now, as Mrs. Osmond, intimately involved with the most distinctive feature of her experience—the evil of the fallen world; in the third she is the mature adult who has successfully passed through the experience and not been defeated by it. She is finally the sum of all she has been— maiden, woman, and heroine: "She had not known where to turn; but she knew now." We have seen the sequence of events, all right, and now we see—thanks to the technique of framing—not only the achieved result but, as though at the same time, those events that produced it, the finished, unified, complete *Portrait of a Lady.*

Notes and References

1. "The Art of Fiction," in *Literary Criticism*, vol. 1, *Essays on Literature, American Writers, English Writers*, ed. Leon Edel and Mark Wilson (New York: Library of America, 1984), 53; hereafter cited in the text as *Criticism*.

2. Alfred Habegger, *Gender, Fantasy, and Realism in American Fiction* (New York: Columbia University Press, 1982), viii.

3. Annette T. Rubinstein, "Henry James, American Novelist; or, Isabel Archer, Emerson's Grand-Daughter," in *Weapons of Criticism: Marxism in America and the Literary Tradition*, ed. Norman Rudich (Palo Alto, Calif.: Ramparts Press, 1976), 314; hereafter cited in the text as Rubinstein.

4. Anne T. Margolis, *Henry James and the Problem of the Audience: An International Act* (Ann Arbor, Mich.: UMI Research Press, 1985), 52.

5. An instructive illustration of this development and proliferation is given in John Carlos Rowe's impressive *The Theoretical Dimensions of Henry James* (Madison: University of Wisconsin Press, 1984). Although it has little to say about *The Portrait of a Lady* specifically and is in fact not at all easy reading, Rowe's book shows how a variety of current critical approaches—literary influence, feminism, psychoanalysis, Marxism, phenomenology, and reader response—contribute to an appreciation of James's work.

6. Judith Fryer, *The Faces of Eve: Women in the Nineteenth-Century American Novel* (New York: Oxford University Press, 1976), 141–42. See also Gordon Pirie, *Henry James* (London: Evans Brothers, 1974), 79–80, and Elizabeth Jean Sabiston, *The Prison of Womanhood: Four Provincial Heroines in Nineteenth-Century Fiction* (London: Macmillan, 1987), 137.

7. For a brief discussion of this categorization, see the end of chapter 6.

8. See my discussion of this idea at the end of chapter 6.

9. Paul B. Armstrong, *The Phenomenology of Henry James* (Chapel Hill and London: University of North Carolina Press, 1983), 99; hereafter cited in the text.

10. Virginia C. Fowler, *James's American Girl: The Embroidery on the Canvas* (Madison: University of Wisconsin Press, 1984), 35; hereafter cited in the text.

11. From *Moralism and Christianity*, quoted in Frederick H. Young, *The Philosophy of Henry James, Sr.* (New York: Bookman Associates, 1951), 185. We will look again at Fowler's notion that marriage operates "on the level of the universal" later in this chapter.

12. In *Literary Criticism*, vol. 2, *French and Other European Writers, the Prefaces*, ed. Leon Edel and Mark Wilson (New York: Library of America, 1984), 1107–1108.

13. Leo Spitzer, "On the Significance of *Don Quixote*" (1962), in *Cervantes: A Collection of Critical Essays,* ed. Lowry Nelson, Jr. (Englewood Cliffs, N.J.: Prentice-Hall, 1969), 88.

14. Dorothy Van Ghent, *The English Novel: Form and Function* (New York: Rinehart, 1953), 212, and Arnold Kettle, *An Introduction to the English Novel* (London: Hutchinson, 1953), 2, 19. And we have already noted Fowler's use of the term "the tree of knowledge," and might further note the phraseology of her explanation of how Isabel's "ability to grasp the significance of the European experience—and, in James's mind, the significance of human life itself—depended on her capacity to see possible 'abysses' and thereby, of course, to become afraid of falling into them" (39; the fear accompanies mature recognition of the dangers in the objective world); Fowler here echoes the language and repeats the setting of Blake's *Book of Thel:* Thel is drawn out to look into the "abyss" of the fallen world, is terrified by what she sees, and flees howling back to her realm of innocence.

15. Martha Banta, *Henry James and the Occult* (Bloomington: Indiana University Press, 1972), 171; hereafter cited in the text.

16. Fowler comes very near to this recognition when she observes that "'Enrichment of consciousness' can be acquired, clearly, only through the experience of 'a defeat,' 'a mistake,' or 'a shame or two'—for these constitute the 'banquet' of life. This interpretation is the central myth which Isabel creates in order to make life bearable" (79). The quoted words in her first sentence are James's (from *The Portrait*), but the idea is surely Lacanian: that embracing the suffering that attends on grasping knowledge of the world, of the objective Other, is the necessary accompaniment of the move to maturity.

17. Pushing back one's skirts (in the days when ladies wore long skirts, as did Isabel) is a gesture of avoiding something unpleasant, dirty, threatening. I add this piece of perhaps superfluous information because I have found at least one critic (who shall remain unidentified) who has seriously misunderstood the image, considering it to mean "push *up* her skirts"!

18. See also Sabiston, *Prison*, 128. Rubinstein comes close to suggesting that Ralph Touchett is the real Emersonian in the novel.

Selected Bibliography

Primary Works

The Portrait of a Lady: An Authoritative Text. Edited by Robert D. Bamberg.
   New York: W. W. Norton, 1975.
The Complete Notebooks of Henry James. Edited by Leon Edel and Lyall H.
   Powers. New York: Oxford University Press, 1987.
Literary Criticism. Edited by Leon Edel and Mark Wilson. Vol. 1, *Essays on
   Literature, American Writers, English Writers.* Vol. 2, *French and Other
   European Writers, the Prefaces.* New York: Library of America, 1984.
Henry James Letters. Edited by Leon Edel. 4 vols. Cambridge: Harvard Uni-
   versity Press, 1974–84.

Secondary Works

Books

Armstrong, Paul B. *The Phenomenology of Henry James.* Chapel Hill and
   London: University of North Carolina Press, 1983. A phenomenological
   reading enables Armstrong to argue that Isabel must develop a mature
   conception of freedom, which involves recognition of the limitations in
   life.
Berland, Alwyn. *Culture and Conduct in the Novels of Henry James.* Cambridge and London: Cambridge University Press, 1981. Noting James's
   similarity to Arnold, Pater, and Ruskin in identifying civilization and culture, Berland argues that Isabel's quest is for ideal culture, "the study of
   perfection in art and in conduct."
Boone, Joseph Allen. *Tradition Counter Tradition: Love and the Form of*

111

Fiction. Chicago: University of Chicago Press, 1987. Boone locates the 1881 version of *The Portrait* in the tradition of fiction that follows the patriarchical view that marriage is the only viable means of fulfillment for a woman. He might have found that the revised version offers a countertraditional statement denying that marriage is a proper resolution—as he finds in *The Golden Bowl.*

Fowler, Virginia C. *Henry James's American Girl: The Embroidery on the Canvas.* Madison: University of Wisconsin Press, 1984. Adapting the theories of Jacques Lacan on the development of the child, Fowler sees the novel as tracing Isabel's growth from immaturity to maturity through her recognizing the challenge of the "Other"—the world as it actually is; she also sees the importance, almost the necessity, of Isabel's marriage to Osmond.

Fryer, Judith. *The Faces of Eve: Women in the Nineteenth-Century American Novel.* New York: Oxford University Press, 1976. Isabel Archer, one of James's "American Princesses," prelapsarian and Emersonian, is seen as facing choices limited to prospective husbands—her inherited fortune does not give her *absolute* freedom; she finally chooses to return to Osmond and "her self-made prison."

Holland, Laurence B. *The Expense of Vision: Essays on the Craft of Henry James.* Princeton, N.J.: Princeton University Press, 1964. Holland provides a useful interpretive explanation of James's preface and its relevance to *The Portrait.* He notes that James has adapted the plots of J. G. Lockhart's *Adam Blair* and Hawthorne's *Scarlet Letter* to focus on the institution of marriage—not a settled institutional mold, in James's novel, "but a form in the process of being shaped"—and to relate monetary transactions to marital, parental, and aesthetic concerns. He sees Isabel as finally "a victim of her world (including her own temperament and illusions) and of the *Portrait* which creates and paints her."

Kettle, Arnold. *An Introduction to the English Novel,* vol. 2. London: Hutchinson, 1953. Kettle examines the relationship of the themes of wealth and marriage and their connection with that of freedom; though he glimpses *The Portrait*'s links with Milton's *Paradise Lost,* Kettle's ideological bent obliges him to condemn James's "bourgeois" view of freedom.

King, Jeannette. *Tragedy in the Victorian Novel: Theory and Practice in the Novels of George Eliot, Thomas Hardy, and Henry James.* Cambridge: Cambridge University Press, 1978. King sees *The Portrait* as a tragic novel, considers the problem of determinism and free will as related to the concerns of classical and Shakespearean models, and places James's works in the tradition of the tragic fiction of Eliot and Hardy.

Krook, Dorothea. *The Ordeal of Consciousness in Henry James.* New York: Cambridge University Press, 1962. *The Portrait* employs one of James's greatest and most persistent themes, the conflict between the aesthetic and the moral attitude. Krook also looks at the sexual theme; she finds that neither Osmond nor Isabel alters much during the course of the novel.

Long, Robert. *The Great Succession: Henry James and the Legacy of Hawthorne.* Pittsburgh, Pa.: Pittsburgh University Press, 1979. Argues for Hawthorne's influence as visible in James's use (in *The Portrait*) of the English garden and the setting of Rome as appropriate scenes for Isabel's innocence and fallen condition—"the great dramatic chiaroscuro."

Margolis, Anne T. *Henry James and the Problem of the Audience: An International Act.* Ann Arbor, Mich.: UMI Research Press, 1985. Margolis clearly shows that James's most demanding fiction (including *The Portrait*) was an attempt to reach both the hypersophisticated and the "simple" reader—who preferred popular novels—by adapting the conventions of the popular writers and "improving" on them. She sees the ending of *The Portrait* as a good example of James's avoiding both the Anglo-Saxon happy ending and the French "indecent" adulterous ending.

Mull, Donald L. *Henry James's "Sublime Economy": Money as Symbolic Center in the Fiction.* Middletown, Conn.: Wesleyan University Press, 1973. Emphasizes the importance of Isabel's inheritance as her "envelope of circumstances" and the problem of what she will do with it; *The Portrait* is the earliest of James's examinations of the cash nexus.

Pirie, Gordon. *Henry James.* London: Evans Brothers, 1974. Pirie offers a concise, workmanlike review of traditional readings of *The Portrait,* touching on the theme of the emancipation of women and the novel's broader concern with human freedom generally; but he does not directly face the problem of the conclusion of the novel.

Poirier, Richard. *The Comic Sense of Henry James: A Study of the Early Novels.* New York: Oxford University Press, 1960. A careful look at the relationship between "limitations or fixities . . . of the world and the freedom of response and aspiration which innocence allows." Poirier rightly feels that freedom finally means for Isabel that she need feel responsible "only to the good opinion she can have of herself and not to the judgment of anyone else," but thinks that the novel does not sufficiently develop Isabel's idea of freedom.

Sabiston, Elizabeth Jean. *The Prison of Womanhood: Four Provincial Heroines in Nineteenth-Century Fiction.* London: Macmillan, 1987. Chapter 5, "Isabel Archer: the Architect of Consciousness" (114–38) gives a very good reading of the career of the heroine of *The Portrait,* and is particularly astute on James's handling of Isabel's Emersonianism—James "deprecates Emerson's aesthetic blindness as well as his blindness to evil"—and on the significance of the ending of the novel—Isabel "is spiritually free and launched on a life of fine perception. . . . she chooses, of her own free will, to remain in the visibly fallen world of continental Europe."

Torgovnick, Marianna. *Closure in the Novel*. Princeton, N.J.: Princeton University Press, 1981. Discusses helpfully James's substitution of "his own private conventions" for the traditional endings of popular fiction, and considers the new emphasis given the ending by his revisions.

Van Ghent, Dorothy. *The English Novel: Form and Function*. New York: Holt, Rinehart & Winston, 1953. One of the very best of earlier Jamesian critics, Van Ghent discusses the themes of freedom versus necessity, of the role of money, and of the necessity to learn to distinguish between good and evil, and makes an illuminating connection between James and the Miltonic tradition.

Veeder, William. *Henry James: The Lesson of the Master: Popular Fiction and Personal Style in the Nineteenth Century*. Chicago and London: University of Chicago Press, 1975. A most thorough canvasing of the relationship of James's early fiction (including *The Portrait*) to the popular fiction of his contemporaries, which permits Veeder several perceptive comments on Isabel's career and particularly on the complexity of Isabel's final decisions; and although he regrettably subscribes to the notion that Isabel fears sexuality, he correctly explains that her return to Rome is not simply "the triumph of duty over the powers of sexuality," that Caspar is really only offering "to lead her back into the world of stage roles": "Isabel has moved beyond her need for Male-as-Protector, and has become at last her own guide."

Wagenknecht, Edward. *Eve and Henry James: Portraits of Women and Girls in his Fiction*. Norman: University of Oklahoma Press, 1978. The chapter on Isabel Archer is a sane, commonsensical, and very well-informed review of her career. Wagenknecht has read everything (footnotes are rich, varied, far-ranging) and dispenses rough justice to other critics. A mind-clearing breath of fresh air: Isabel's final decision is inevitable, given her development through the novel, and she has no other real options.

Ward, Joseph A. *The Imagination of Disaster: Evil in the Fiction of Henry James*. Lincoln: University of Nebraska Press, 1961. Ward's careful reading distinguishes *The Portrait*'s use of the biblical story of man's fall, considers Isabel's experience "fortunate," and rightly claims some inevitability about her final decision. Offers a perceptive evaluation of Osmond.

Weinstein, Philip M. *Henry James and the Requirements of the Imagination*. Cambridge: Harvard University Press, 1971. A useful explication of *The Portrait* as an example of psychological realism, justifying the typical Jamesian absence of "action" and "adventure" by emphasis on the fact that for James "seeing . . . is doing."

Selected Bibliography

Essays

Collections

Perspectives on James's "The Portrait of a Lady": A Collection of Critical Essays. Edited by William T. Stafford. New York: New York University Press; London: London University Press, 1967.

Twentieth Century Interpretations of "The Portrait of a Lady": A Collection of Critical Essays. Edited by Peter Buitenhuis. Englewood Cliffs, N.J.: Prentice-Hall, 1968.

Studies in "The Portrait of a Lady." Edited by Lyall H. Powers. Columbus, Ohio: Charles E. Merrill, 1970.

"New Essays on *The Portrait of a Lady*." Edited by Daniel Mark Fogel. *Henry James Review* 7 (1986).

Henry James's "The Portrait of a Lady": Modern Critical Interpretations. Edited by Harold Bloom. New York: Chelsea House, 1987.

Individual Essays

Baym, Nina. "Revision and Thematic Change in *The Portrait of a Lady*." *Modern Fiction Studies* 22 (1976): 183–200. Baym expresses a distinct preference for the 1881 version of *The Portrait* and establishes the creation of Isabel Archer as an important contribution to the examination of "the woman question"; Baym distinguishes provocatively between the concerns of 1881—awareness is a means to achieving independence—and of 1908—independence is attained only in awareness; "the two things are almost identical."

Benert, Annette Larson. "The Dark Source of Love: A Jungian Reading of Two Early James Novels." *University of Hartford Studies in Literature* 2 (1980): 99–123. Benert applies Jungian theories of nature and psyche in an attempt to clarify some aspects of *The Portrait.*

Buitenhuis, Peter. "Americans in European Gardens." *Henry James Review* 7 (1986): 124–30. Strengthens understanding of the metaphoric quality of the international theme; expands on Long's study of Hawthorne's influence, especially that of "Rappaccini's Daughter," showing how the garden imagery extends to all principals and particularly to Goodwood's final appeal.

Djwa, Sandra. "*Ut Pictura Poesis:* The Making of a Lady." *Henry James Review* 7 (1986): 72–85. Drawing on indications of influence on James from such as Eliot, Browning, and Pater, Djwa explains how Isabel's progress from innocence through experience gives her moral as distinct from aesthetic knowledge and leads her to the final decision: "she has evolved her own standards of life and morality . . . is now a woman of developed sensibility, the 'lady' of the title."

Edel, Leon. "Introduction" (v–xx). *The Portrait of a Lady*. Boston: Houghton Mifflin, 1956. In a seminal introduction to the novel, covering its provenance, the originals of principal characters, and its artistic achievement, Edel places Isabel in the gallery of literary heroines and beside the "new woman" in her quest for freedom.

———. "The Myth of America in *The Portrait of a Lady*." *Henry James Review* 7 (1986): 8–17. Places *The Portrait* accurately in the stream of literary history and of the history of the United States as well as in James's career; develops the Emersonian quality of Isabel—"James is quietly undermining the Emersonian doctrine . . . 'Trust thyself'"; presents a detailed claim for Isabel as a representative American, and for the novel as "half-consciously" prophetic of America's destiny.

Fischer, Sandra K. "Isabel Archer and the Enclosed Chamber." *Henry James Review* 7 (1986): 48–58. Having determined that *The Portrait* ends with Isabel's walking into the house at Gardencourt (away from Goodwood), Fischer applies "the metaphor of enclosed space . . . proposed by Gaston Bachelard" to her reading of the novel and concludes that finally "Isabel has accepted her entrapment." Those who, like Henrietta Stackpole, believe that Isabel has *come out* of the house at Gardencourt, subsequently, to return to Rome may find this reading unsatisfactory though ingenious.

Johnson, Courtney. "Adam and Eve and Isabel Archer." *Renascence* 21 (1969): 134–44, 167. Proposes the biblical story of man's fall and redemption as the informing source of *The Portrait*; explains Isabel's final attitude as similar to St. Augustine's "well-directed love"; and properly locates carnal love—not antagonistic to human integrity—in the novel's schema.

Krause, Sydney J. "James's Revisions of the Style of *The Portrait of a Lady*." *American Literature* 30 (1958): 67–88. Indicates that James's intention in his revision of the novel was to clarify the intentions of the original version, and that the author was "making a consistent effort to gain greater clarity and concreteness."

Matthiessen, F. O. "The Painter's Sponge and the Varnish Bottle" (1944). Pp. 577–97 of the Norton Critical Edition of *The Portrait of a Lady*. Edited by Robert D. Bamberg. An early, detailed study of James's revisions of *The Portrait*, arguing that James's intentions were to clarify and improve his novel: "The growth from ideas to images is what James had been fumbling for" and led to his making the 1908 version more concrete and more dramatic. Yet Matthiessen concludes that Isabel remains "essentially virginal" and "afraid of sexual possession," and that she returns to Rome out of a sense of duty—to Osmond.

Mazzella, Anthony J. "The New Isabel." Pp. 597–619 of *The Portrait*, ed.

Selected Bibliography

Bamberg. Confirms but goes beyond the best of the earlier studies of revision: demonstrates that the revised text is more "imagistic" and that the new Isabel has "a significantly expanded consciousness"; shows that increased emphasis is given to Isabel's "freedom and vulnerability" and that her final decision is motivated by fear "that her freedom will be lost through [surrender to Goodwood's] erotic possession."

Niemtzow, Annette. "Marriage and the New Woman in *The Portrait of a Lady*." *American Literature* 47 (1975): 377–95. Compares the attitudes implicit in *The Portrait* to the published ideas on marriage and divorce of James's father, and understands the "open-ended" quality of the novel as James's move "from the marriage novel to the verge of the divorce novel . . . an aesthetic commitment in consonance with newly visible nineteenth-century social reality."

Powers, Lyall H. "*The Portrait of a Lady:* 'The Eternal Mystery of Things.'" *Nineteenth-Century Fiction* 14 (1959): 143–55. Argues that Isabel's career follows the pattern of the "Fortunate Fall," without suggesting that the novel is any strict sense religious.

———. "Visions and Revisions: The Past Rewritten." *Henry James Review* 7 (1986): 105–16. Accounts for the nature of the 1908 revisions of *The Portrait* and their significance by reference to a congeries of events that occurred in James's life in the quarter century between the two versions— especially his return to Newport and the revived memories of Minny Temple and his friendship with Hendrik Andersen. Finds the ending clarified in terms of its affirmation of Isabel's right decision.

Rahv, Philip. "The Heiress of All the Ages." *Image and Idea: Fourteen Essays on Literary Themes*. New York: New Directions, 1949. One of the earliest studies to broach the idea of the metaphoric nature of James's international theme—Isabel and the problem of innocence and experience. Sees Isabel as an Emersonian creation.

Rubinstein, Annette T. "Henry James, American Novelist; or, Isabel Archer, Emerson's Grand-Daughter." Pp. 311–26 of *Weapons of Criticism: Marxism in America and the Literary Tradition*. Edited by Norman Rudich. Palo Alto, Calif.: Ramparts Press, 1976. Convincingly places James as author of *The Portrait* in the tradition of Cooper, Hawthorne, and Melville, as "an abstract or metaphysical novelist . . . of pure poetry" rather than a traditional realist—an important observation. Discusses Isabel and the question of freedom as an Emersonian matter—very persuasively.

Sabiston, Elizabeth. "The Architect of Consciousness and the International Theme." *Henry James Review* 7 (1986): 29–47. Drawing on her own *Prison of Womanhood* to place Isabel in the tradition of "Emma's Daughters," Sabiston indicates her place in the Hawthorne tradition of the "fortunate fall" as well and thus recognizes the important choice Isabel makes at the end of the novel as a refusal to flee the actual, fallen world.

Shriber, Mary S. "Isabel Archer and Victorian Manners." *Studies in the Novel* 8 (1976): 441–57. Situates *The Portrait* within the Victorian context and thus accounts for the apparent conflict between the Victorian idea of "the lady" and the demands of the "new woman."

Stafford, William T. "*The Portrait of a Lady:* The Second Hundred Years." *Henry James Review* 2 (1981): 91–100. On the hundredth anniversary of the first version of *The Portrait,* Stafford "predicts" that new developments in criticism of the novel will include recognition of chapter 47 as a crucial moment in the novel, that Henrietta Stackpole will be taken more seriously, and that Isabel's "highly comedic" role will be re-evaluated.

———. "The Enigma of Serena Merle." *Henry James Review* 7 (1986): 117–23. A review of critical response to Madame Merle, including the "white-blackbird" idea, the association of her with Niobe and Juno, and attempts to do fuller justice to this somewhat underrated artistic creation, who is "problematic, to be sure, fallible, certainly, but, above all, enigmatically and believably human."

Tanner, Tony. "The Fearful Self: Henry James's *The Portrait of a Lady.*" *Critical Quarterly* 7 (1965): 205–219. In an excellent essay Tanner incidentally anticipates and corrects many subsequent (and persistent) misreadings of *The Portrait*. He explains how the novel traces the psychic quest for self-discovery, and presents Isabel's career as "emblematic": James has so selected and arranged his realistic data, and has "so saturated it with deeper implications" as to present a quest "which far transcends the social realism." Defines the moral attitude of the novel by adapting Kantian terms to the reading—such as the distinction between "value" and "worth," and the moral imperative to treat human beings as ends rather than as means—and concludes that Isabel has finally "seen through the false aesthetic approach to life" and "now appreciates the true artistic attitude"—that is, the Jamesian *moral* attitude. Isabel "has started to become a Jamesian artist": her quest ends in her gaining a clear vision and liberation from dominance by deception—a positive ending to the novel.

Templeton, Wayne. "*The Portrait of a Lady:* A Question of Freedom." *English Studies in Canada* 7 (1981): 312–28. Sees Isabel's quest for freedom in social and philosophical terms, and deems the quest successful because she has encountered reality pragmatically and has rejected her initially romantic attitude.

Tintner, Adeline R. "Pater in *The Portrait of a Lady* and *The Golden Bowl,* Including Some Unpublished Letters." *Henry James Review* 3 (1982): 80–95. The influence of Pater's *Studies in the History of the Renaissance* is seen in James's rejection of the passivity of Pater's aesthetic philosophy through his characterization of Gilbert Osmond.

Selected Bibliography

———. "Henry James's Debt to George Meredith." *AB Bookman's Weekly* 70 (1982): 1811–27. Finds several meaningful similarities between Meredith's *Egoist* and James's *Portrait,* especially between the characters of Sir Willoughby Patterne and Gilbert Osmond.

———. "'In the Dusky, Crowded, Heterogeneous Back-Shop of the Mind': The Iconography of *The Portrait of a Lady.*" *Henry James Review* 7 (1986): 140–57. Illustrates the function of works of art and "works of utility treated as works of art" as "a major element of James's craft"—for example, that while Ralph identifies himself humorously with a figure in a Watteau painting, he also makes the counterstatement of the novel, "which is the essential critique of the aesthetic point of view." Tintner explains how James's experience in the twenty-five years between the two versions of *The Portrait* accounts for differences in the use of the iconography; both versions use the icons artistically: "Far from surface decorations, they are integral to the firm structure of the novel."

Torsney, Cheryl B. "The Political Context of *The Portrait of a Lady.*" *Henry James Review* 7 (1986): 86–104. Argues that James's attitude to the imperialism of Disraeli and the liberalism of Gladstone is reflected in his characterizations of Osmond and Warburton, respectively, and further that the revised version's reemphasis on his anti-imperialism is a result of his experience of twentieth-century U.S. imperialism.

White, Robert. "Love, Marriage, and Divorce: The Matter of Sexuality in *The Portrait of a Lady.*" *Henry James Review* 7 (1986): 59–71. White's suggestion that we understand attitudes to love, marriage, and divorce in *The Portrait* in terms of Henry James, Sr.'s published ideas leads to the helpful argument that Isabel is not repelled by Goodwood's kiss but "terrified by an awareness of her own sexuality" and the "power of the passion that has all but engulfed them, an awful power," and that even Osmond's appeal "in its very subtlety and delicacy is decidedly sexual."

Wiesenfarth, Joseph. "A Woman in *The Portrait of a Lady.*" *Henry James Review* 7 (1986): 18–28. *The Portrait* asks "how a woman does justice to her *self*" in terms of the posed opposition of Ralph and Osmond; it shows us, in a literally verbal portrait, Isabel as a girl and, later, as a lady, but finally as a woman who has found her *self*—made one "with the girl and the lady."

Bibliographic Aids

Cargill, Oscar. "*The Portrait of a Lady.*" Pp. 78–119 of *The Novels of Henry James*. New York: Macmillan, 1961. A thorough review of critical and scholarly treatments of *The Portrait* to 1960, with valuable footnotes.

Foley, Richard N. *"The Portrait of a Lady."* Pp. 26–30 of *Criticism in American Periodicals of the Works of Henry James from 1866 to 1916.* Washington, D.C.: Catholic University of America Press, 1944.

Gard, Roger. *"The Portrait of a Lady."* Pp. 93–147 of *Henry James: The Critical Heritage.* London: Routledge & Kegan Paul; New York: Barnes & Noble, 1968.

Richmond, Marion. "The Early Critical Reception of *The Portrait of a Lady* (1881–1916)." *Henry James Review* 7 (1986): 158–63.

———. "Henry James's *The Portrait of a Lady:* A Bibliography of Primary Material and Annotated Criticism." *Henry James Review* 7 (1986): 164–95.

Wagenknecht, Edward. "Achievement: *The Portrait of a Lady.*" Pp. 76–96 of *The Novels of Henry James.* New York: Frederick Ungar, 1983. A review essay of the critical and scholarly approaches to *The Portrait* with a brisk evaluation of each; contains a broad range of footnotes. Supplements Cargill.

Index

Index

The Author

Lyall H. Powers, now Professor of English at the University of Michigan, was born and raised in Canada. He was educated at the University of Winnipeg (B.A. Hons.), the University of Manitoba (M.A.), the Sorbonne, and Indiana University (Ph.D.). He served with the Royal Canadian Air Force and the Canadian Army. He has taught at the University of Manitoba, Indiana University, the University of Wisconsin, the University of British Columbia, the University of Göttingen, and the University of Hawaii in Manoa. His books and articles on English, American, Canadian, and French literature include *Henry James and the Naturalist Movement, Henry James: An Introduction and Interpretation,* and *Faulkner's Yoknapatawpha Comedy;* he has edited *The Portable Henry James* (revised), *Studies in "The Portrait of a Lady", Henry James's Major Novels: Essays in Criticism, Leon Edel and Literary Art,* and *Henry James and Edith Wharton: Letters 1900–1915,* and with Leon Edel, *"Henry James and the Bazar Letters"* and *The Complete Notebooks of Henry James.* He is a member of the editorial board of the *Henry James Review* and treasurer of the Margaret Laurence International Society. In 1986 he was elected a fellow of the Royal Society of Arts. He is currently preparing a literary biography of Canadian novelist Margaret Laurence.